TWO PLAYS

Sarah Woods

TWO PLAYS

GRACE
CAKE
from a collaboration with Jade

with an introduction
by David Edgar

OBERON BOOKS
LONDON

First published in 2003 by Oberon Books Ltd.
(incorporating Absolute Classics)
521 Caledonian Road, London N7 9RH
Tel: 020 7607 3637 / Fax: 020 7607 3629
e-mail: oberon.books@btinternet.com
www.oberonbooks.com

A catalogue record for this book is available from the British Library.

ISBN: 1 84002 425 9

Cover design: Andrzej Klimowski

Contents

For Poppy, Lillian and Saul – my wonderful spoons.

Introduction

I first met Sarah Woods in a union meeting. People have forgotten how important the Theatre Writers' Union was in creating the network of playwrights' self-help institutions – bodies like North West Playwrights and later Stagecoach in the west midlands, countless workshops, short courses and reading groups – which led to the upsurge of new theatre writing in Britain in the mid-1990s. Think of that upsurge, and you probably picture a young man writing sexually-explicit plays about the crisis of masculinity, performed at the Royal Court Theatre Upstairs and then all around Europe. You could just as well think about a young woman, going on a writers' course, starting out in community or small scale theatre, maybe founding their own company and certainly adept at collaborating with other people's, now making a tidy living writing a wide variety of work for a wide variety of performance media. Sarah Woods is a good example of this kind of writer.

When we met she was applying to go on a post-graduate playwriting course I'd just founded at the University of Birmingham; without a first degree, the university insisted she be classed as an 'occasional' student (in reality, as 'occasional' as Virgin Trains are 'occasionally' delayed). Now, fourteen years later, she is running the course herself, which says all that needs to be said about that.

The play she wrote on the course – *Nervous Women* – was set in two timescales, one contemporary, one in the past, anticipating the epidemic of plays on this model which was to erupt a few years later. Since then, Woods has produced a body of work in a number of different media and theatre forms, which mix media and styles (she has created a striking series of radio works melding documentary, drama and music), often involving open and equal collaboration with other artists.

The two plays in this book – written for Victoria Worsley's company Jade – are excellent examples of this strand. Both plays have the work of other artists built into their very structure – Worsley herself as performer, but also designers and (for *Cake*) puppeteers. But neither could have been written by anyone else.

Grace and *Cake* are contests between two women and their surroundings. In *Grace*, the woman is about to be thirty, her life situation outlined with wonderful economy in her erratically-ordered list of morning tasks ('Tidy room. Hoover. Sort out washing. Fix cupboard door. Put up shelves. Have a child. Make some tea. Get out of bed.'). In *Cake*, the woman has two children and is discovered at her kitchen worktop demonstrating the making of a Victoria Sponge. In both cases, a world of relative order is disrupted by invasions: in *Grace*, from a series of real, imaginary and mythic males emerging from cupboards; in *Cake*, by a set of wooden spoons, animated by two visible but spookily expressionless puppeteers, later joined by a faintly sinister and certainly uppity speaking doll, who not only disrupts the cake-making procedure but also challenges the very aim and purpose of the art. Of course, the mythic males represent the actual males that invade and disrupt Grace's life, and, sure, the spoons are kids. But they are also theatrical images which make Grace and Mum's inner lives visible and as such do the same job as the Greek chorus, the Shakespearian soliloquy and the restoration aside.

What is remarkable about these images is not just their technical skill and wit but the way that they are integrated with the language of the monologues which surround them and which – increasingly – they disrupt. Woods is adept at expressing the mounting panic of women feeling their life slipping out of control. She also relishes the vocabularies of the worlds through which her characters move – from the increasingly staccato lists that snake through *Grace*, via the jargon of an incomprehensibly articulate DIY man to the recipes that form the spine of *Cake*. (There is a real passion in her description of the essential physics of cake-making, described in charming if insistent detail, even as the wayward spoons move in). Innovative when *Grace* was written, the world of either-side-of-thirty female angst has become a familiar one for novelists and playwrights alike. But whenever we feel comfortable in the territory, Woods rings an emotional change, or, more accurately, exposes an emotional truth, that could not exist outside the theatrical device. The moment when – attacked by all the forces of chaos on all sides – Mum defends the making and eating of cake as a ceremony without which her family could not and would not exist, suddenly invests a comic image with deep, echoing meaning.

By definition, these plays are completed fully only in performance; but Woods' work challenges the idea that collaborative playmaking implies thin and featureless writing. *Grace* and *Cake* are a joy in the theatre but also a rich pleasure on the page.

David Edgar
October, 2003

GRACE

Notes

A forward slashmark / is used to indicate where characters speak at the same time as one another. This usually applies to immediately consecutive speeches unless otherwise stated in the stage directions.

Characters

GRACE

ANDREY

CENTAURS

CENTURION

DARCY

MARK ANTHONY

DOCTOR

DIY MAN

CLASSICAL MUSIC MEN

BIRD

BABY

DOG

Grace was first performed by Jade Theatre Company at The Tron Theatre, Glasgow on 24 July 1997, with the following cast:

GRACE, Victoria Worsley

CENTAUR / DARCY / MAGICIAN / DIY MAN, Richard Clothier

CENTAUR / MARK ANTHONY / CHIP / DOCTOR, Robin Pirongs

Other parts were performed by Robin Pirongs and Richard Clothier.

Director, Theresa Heskins

Designer, Nigel Prabhavalkar

Lighting Designer, Charles Balfour

Composer, Anders Sodergren

Jade was founded in 1992 by Victoria Worsley to bridge the gap between physical / visual theatre and new writing. Its unique combination combines the inventiveness and theatricality of physical / visual work with the rigour, structure and depth of a written text.

GRACE's room. There are lots of cupboards, including a wardrobe. On the floor is a rug, a newspaper, a glass, a half-empty bottle of wine and a part-finished game of patience. GRACE is in bed, completely covered by a duvet. There is music. It is getting light. On top of the wardrobe is a clock. Its alarm sounds. The music stops. The music starts again. The alarm sounds again.

A pair of eyes peep out from under the duvet.

GRACE: Tidy room.
　Hoover.
　Sort out washing.
　Fix cupboard door.
　Put up shelves.
　Have a child.
　Make some tea.
　Get out of bed.
　(*A moment. Can she? She retreats back under the duvet, curls up into a little ball.*
　Silence, then:)
　Buy: pasta, lettuce, cheese, olives, bread, Ultra Bra, baked beans, washing-up liquid.
　Cut nails.
　Eat.
　Breathe.
　(*She breathes out, then in – slowly, trying not to panic.*)
　Get up.
　(*She gets up.*)
　Get fit.
　Learn Russian.
　Decide what to wear.
　(*She opens the wardrobe, leafs through her clothes and takes something out. As she continues, she dresses.*)
　Phone mum.
　Phone bank.
　Put wash on.
　Back up computer discs.
　Pay Visa bill.
　Get married.

Set video.

Listen to classical music.

Wash hair.

Swim the channel.

(*She is dressed, but doesn't like the effect. She undresses.*)

Get into a steady relationship.

Do lottery syndicate.

Unload washing.

(*She goes to a cupboard, opens it, washing pours out as though from a washing machine.*)

Read reports.

Find a man.

(*She picks up the washing.*)

Get promoted.

Decide what to wear.

(*She goes to the wardrobe, opens it, dumps the washing inside and shuts the door.*)

Iron clothes.

(*She opens a cupboard to reveal a tin of paint.*)

Paint skirting board.

(*She takes out the pot of paint and walks with it.*)

Phone mum.

Back up computer discs.

(*She puts the paint down.*)

Make a cup of tea.

(*She goes to another cupboard and takes out a kettle – from behind it, DARCY stares. GRACE doesn't notice.*)

Hoover.

Paint skirting board.

Phone mum.

Listen to classical music.

(*She opens another cupboard. Classical music plays from it and inside A MUSIC MAN wearing a dickie-bow conducts. She decides not to believe her eyes and shuts the cupboard. As she continues, she puts down the kettle and folds the duvet.*)

Read reports.

Hoover.

Learn Russian.

(She opens a cupboard to put the duvet in, to reveal ANDREY, a 'Learn Russian in Five Minutes' man.)

ANDREY: Bol-shoi pohov-ye ajye-yala.

(She gives him the duvet.)

GRACE: Bol-shoi pohov-ye ajye-yala.

ANDREY: Duvet.

GRACE: Put out milk bottles.

Put out rubbish.

Put out cat.

ANDREY: Mas-la.

(She starts doing exercises.)

GRACE: Get a cat.

ANDREY: Mas-la.

GRACE: Mas-la.

ANDREY: Butter.

GRACE: Buy.

ANDREY: Ma-la-ko.

GRACE: Ma-la-ko.

ANDREY: Milk.

GRACE: Pasta, lettuce, cheese, olives –

ANDREY: Hlyep.

GRACE: Hlyep.

ANDREY: Bread.

GRACE: Ultra Bra.

ANDREY: Ultra Bra.

(She shuts the Russian cupboard and picks up the kettle.)

GRACE: Make a cup of tea.

(She opens a cupboard to put the kettle in – the same washing falls out.)

Do ironing.

(She takes the washing out. Puts the kettle in. She opens a cupboard – inside the classical music plays and both MUSIC MEN play instruments. She shuts the cupboard.)

Have children.

(The clock ticks – it reads eight o'clock.)

Give birth.

(She puts the paint pot into a cupboard, shuts it.)

Get pregnant.

Learn Russian.
(*She opens another cupboard to put washing inside – ANDREY is there.*)
ANDREY: Zdnyom razh-dye-nee-ya.
GRACE: Zdnyom razh-dye-nee-ya.
Do washing.
(*She opens another cupboard. From inside DARCY stares – she doesn't notice. She bungs the washing in.*)
ANDREY: Happy Birthday.
GRACE: Get dressed.
ANDREY: Bi-strye-ya.
GRACE: Bi-strye-ya.
ANDREY: Quicker.
(*She slams the Russian cupboard.*)
GRACE: Find something to wear.
(*She goes to the wardrobe, inside is only a Regency dress. She takes it out.*)
Listen to classical music.
(*She opens another cupboard – the music plays and A MUSIC MAN speaks as GRACE puts the dress on. To begin with he gestures with his own hand, then his hand disappears and reappears in a distant cupboard.*)
MUSIC MAN: The finale – Allegro molto – opens with another leaping phrase, and the whole movement is –
(*He brings his hand to his mouth to cough, then returns it to the distant cupboard.*)
– characterised by the alternating and contrasting of these abrupt gestures with the flowing melody first announced by the strings.
GRACE: Get married.
(*A cupboard opens to reveal ANDREY.*)
ANDREY: Moosh.
GRACE: Moosh.
ANDREY: Husband.
GRACE: Find a man.
(*She opens the wardrobe – DARCY is inside on his horse. GRACE doesn't see him, but notices the paint pot.*)
ANDREY: Pa-sma-tree-tye.
GRACE: Pa-sma-tree-tye.

(*She picks it up.*)

Paint skirting board.

(*DARCY's musical theme begins. DARCY trots out of the cupboard and stands, his horse a little frisky, not looking at GRACE.*)

ANDREY: Look.

(*GRACE looks at DARCY.*)

Sma-tryety.

GRACE: Sma-tryety.

ANDREY: To look.

(*GRACE shuts the cupboard on ANDREY.*)

GRACE: Can I get you a drink?

(*Still DARCY doesn't look at her.*)

Tea? Coffee? Wine?

(*He gallops off – back through the wardrobe which shuts behind him. A moment.*

She opens the wardrobe.

DARCY has gone. Inside hangs a wedding dress with a huge, long train. Confetti blows out. She takes the Regency dress off.)

He didn't say he didn't love me.

He didn't say there was anyone else in his life.

He didn't say a word.

(*She gets out the dress and puts it on as she continues.*)

He didn't ask me to give up my career.

He didn't say I couldn't get married in white and have a career and have a perfect body and be a virgin and have beautiful children who slide out of my fanny like airmail letters and amuse themselves immediately with some colouring in as I interview for Homes and Gardens, Hello! GQ, Gardeners' World, Vogue, Good Parenting, Here's Health, The Jane Asher magazine and cook dinner parties for twelve while having colonic irrigation.

(*She puts on the train, which continues back into the wardrobe.*)

I will always be at work and always be at the gym and always be at the supermarket and always answer the phone and always meet my kids from school in a Renault Espace.

(*She lowers her head – coy – and starts to walk forward towards the audience. A wedding march plays.*)

This is the day.

This is my day.

I am radiant.

No matter how much of a dog I have looked over the last twenty nine years and eleven months – I am beautiful now.

(*The train catches, pulling her backwards by the head. She stops. Pulls at the train with her head, like a bull. The train gives and she moves forward again.*)

No matter how many times I have shaved my head, no matter how many needles I have stuck through my ears and my nose and my labia – my hair curls and bounces around my shoulders and I am unpierced now.

(*The veil catches but she pulls at it and manages to keep going, her teeth gritted.*)

No matter how many wraps of whizz I have snorted, bucket bongs I have tripped over, no matter how many times I have been dragged from Trafalgar Square screaming – 'You fucking fascist bizzie bastards' –

(*The veil catches again, much harder, almost pulling her over.*)

I am innocent now!

(*She pulls the train with her head, pawing the ground with her feet, until it gives and she can move on.*)

No matter how many German Shepherd fantasies I have had, no matter how many pairs of crotchless panties I have been licked through. No matter how many rimming, fist-fucking nights I have spent –

(*The veil catches, pulling her flat onto her back.*)

I am virginal now!

(*She writhes around, but cannot escape. The more she writhes, the more tangled in the veil she becomes.*)

I will have him.

I will captivate him.

I am irresistible.

I am completely confident in my powers.

They will build a pure gold statue in my honour.

I will be Queen!
I will rule the land!
I will be Queen of Kings.
I will have it all.
My son will be the sun and my daughter will be the moon.
(*A CENTAUR enters.*)
Take me to him!
Carry me to him!
(*He rushes over and picks her up.*)
Take me to him now!
(*He carries her off. The MAGICIAN's spangly music plays as the door of a small, high cupboard opens and the MAGICIAN peeps out. He looks around. He sees that the coast is clear. He motions 'Ssh' to the audience. He scales down a rope or ropeladder to the ground. He motions to the cupboard he has just come out of and a beautifully wrapped present floats out and down, into his hands. He places it in a prominent position. The playing card the Ace of Hearts appears magically in his hand. He shows the audience. The other side is the back of a playing card. He spins the card, the other side now reads 'For Grace'. He tucks it under the ribbon on the present, Ace of Hearts side up, and leaves the way he came.*)
Music for a big song and dance number begins. A spotlight lights a high cupboard. It opens to reveal GRACE. As she begins to sing, she walks down to the ground via a staircase of drawers which open as she descends – perhaps they have fairy lights down their sides. The two CENTAURS enter. As she reaches the bottom, they get on all fours to become her final two steps. She reaches the ground and the CENTAURS dance with macho top halves, but their bottom halves sometimes skip and paw the ground. Sometimes GRACE strokes their furry legs. The dance routine is after Madonna and Marilyn Monroe and includes movements such as: the CENTAURS taking her hands and escorting her round the space, surrounding her and her bursting out of the middle of them. She falls backwards into their arms, is carried horizontally by them. She knocks one of them over and, escorted by the other, puts her foot on his chest. They lift her by her outstretched arms, they lift her

*by the legs so that she towers above them. She touches their
faces and they smile.)*
(*Sings.*) I've been seen in high society
And I've kept bad company.
I've been up, I've been down, I've been spun around,
But none of it mattered to me.

I've been to London and I've seen the Queen,
I've seen every Queen who's ever been.
That was me – in your wildest dreams,
But your too much is never enough.

It will be different this time,
I'm going to a different place.
I know what dress I'm wearing and
What sandwiches I'll take.

I'm heading where the sky meets the sea
I know I'll get there this time.
I'm heading for the beach of my life,
I know I'll have it this time.
(*As GRACE continues, she becomes rougher with the
CENTAURS – pushing them around.*)
I'm gonna have to fly –
Hugs and kisses – bye-bye!
I'm heading where the sky meets the sea.
I'm heading for the beach of my life.
I'm going to find the rainbow's end.
(*As she continues, she hits one of the CENTAURS in the face
– by accident.*)
This time (my time)
I'm here (I am)
It's now (And how)
I'm making waves.
(*The hurt CENTAUR leaves.
The other CENTAUR tries to continue alone, but soon follows
his friend.*)
Stand back (Well back)
Make way (No way)
Step aside (Big step)

(*GRACE is left alone.*)

I'm coming...through.

(*Unsure what to do, she moves over to a cupboard.*)

Through.

(*Opens it.*)

Through.

(*Puts the microphone in. She is saved by the CENTURION who pops his head through a high cupboard.*)

CENTURION: Mark Anthony approaches.

(*He slams the door.*)

GRACE: Mark Anthony.

(*As she continues, she runs around trying to tidy the place.*)

This could be it. This could be the one.

Make a good impression.

Rich. Powerful.

Strong.

Virile.

(*She opens a cupboard to put stuff away, a pile of papers fall out.*)

Quick – quick!

(*She starts to gather them up.*)

Big house. Chariots.

Half the civilised world.

A passionate affair. Get rid of his wife. A few kids.

Yes.

(*A bugle sounds.*)

Yes. Yes.

(*She opens the wardrobe to put some papers in – revealing MARK ANTHONY, a vision of manhood. His musical theme plays.*)

MARK: All of Rome is talking about you.

(*He walks into the room.*)

GRACE: Can I get you a drink?

MARK: I am just returned from the battles of Philipi in Macedonia.

GRACE: Tea? Coffee? Wine?

MARK: Wine.

(*As he continues, she opens the drinks cupboard – and takes out a flask of red wine and two pewter tankards.*)

Ours was an overwhelming victory. I myself ran my sword through three hundred and fifty men.

(*She hands him a glass – he drains it.*)

GRACE: Alexander.

MARK: There may have been an Alexander / among them.

GRACE: What do you think of Alexander?

MARK: Is he a Caesarian?

GRACE: As a name. For a little boy.

(*To herself.*) Perhaps it's too weighty.

MARK: We now have most of the Roman world to ourselves, Marcus Anthonius, Octavian and Lepidus.

GRACE: Cleopatra.

MARK: Lepidus.

GRACE: Cleopatra Selene. If it's a girl.

MARK: Except for one dissident part of Sicily now occupied by that semi-Republican pirate the outlawed Sextus Pompeius. But I suspect Octavian.

GRACE: I've been talking to a dressmaker.

MARK: Talk to no-one. I believe he has some intrigue with that pirate Pompeius.

GRACE: She suggested a sculpted fitted bodice in Duchesse satin with a silk skirt and train.

MARK: No-one is safe.

Cassius and Brutus have lost their lives.

GRACE: I don't believe it.

MARK: Assassinated.

GRACE: Who's going to sit with Flavia and Octavia? The seating plan's a mess.

MARK: I told them to watch their backs.

GRACE: There's always someone getting butchered in his bed.

MARK: As I always watch my back.

GRACE: There just aren't enough single men.

MARK: Even in my sleep.

GRACE: We must book the honeymoon.

MARK: I have taken the Transatlantic Gaul and the Adriatic provinces.

GRACE: What about the Caribbean?

(*He looks at her.*)

Barbados.

MARK: I do not recall Barbados.

GRACE: Lazing on the beach.

MARK: Barbados.

GRACE: Sipping Bacardi.

MARK: I must have Barbados.

GRACE: I can't wait.

MARK: I cannot take you with me.

GRACE: I think it's traditional.

MARK: Too treacherous.

GRACE: Somewhere closer to home, then. Scotland?

MARK: Not even I dare –
> (*The cupboard bursts open and the CENTURION pokes his head out.*)

CENTURION: My Lord, the Parthians have launched an invasion of the Roman Empire. Pacoras has descended upon Syria while the Roman renegade Quintus Labienus advances rapidly into Asia Minor.
> (*On finishing, the CENTURION shuts the cupboard.*)

GRACE: Quintus is quite nice.

MARK: I have to sail to Tyre.

GRACE: What about dinner?

MARK: I'll grab a sandwich on the way.
> (*He opens the wardrobe door. The bugle sounds.*)

GRACE: Oh. When will you be back?

MARK: Two. Three years.

CENTURION: (*Off.*) My Lord!
> (*He leaves, shutting the wardrobe door behind him.*
> *GRACE leans against the door, then looks round the room, crestfallen.*)

GRACE: Three years isn't long.
> Tankards.
> (*She picks up the tankards.*)
> Get myself organised.
> (*She drains a tankard.*)
> Tie things up at work.
> (*Drains the second and puts them in the cupboard.*)
> I've got plenty of time.
> Dress.

(She takes the Cleopatra robe off.)
Plenty to do.
Decanter.
(She picks up the decanter.)
Plenty of time.
(She drains the decanter.)
He'll be back before I even notice he's gone.
(As she puts the decanter away, her biological clock ticks deafeningly, the second hand moving relentlessly on. It is nearly nine o'clock, or three quarters of the way round.)
Clock.
(A BIRD puppet pops out of the clock.)
BIRD: Nine o'clock.
GRACE: Nine o'clock.
BIRD: Roman Emperors don't come down in every shower.
(GRACE slams the clock door.)
GRACE: Get things organised.
(She sees the present.)
Present.
Get myself together.
(She takes out the Ace of Hearts, turns it over. As she does, the biological clock moment ends.)
For Grace.
(The card drops to the floor. She undoes the ribbon and opens the box – inside is a spangly leotard. She puts it on. Spangly music plays. The wardrobe door swings open to reveal the MAGICIAN in cape, top hat and gloves, a bird cage containing a pretend dove in one hand.
GRACE presents him.
He gives her the bird cage, she presents it and, walking backwards and smiling, puts it on a hook. Meanwhile, he takes off his gloves, cape and hat, gives them to her.
She shows them to the audience, smiling, puts them somewhere.
As he goes to sit down, a folding chair is passed out of a cupboard to GRACE who unfolds it just as he sits.
She folds down a table, right in front of him: on it are a knife and fork. GRACE gets a plate – shows the audience that it's solid. A glass. Once she has put the plate down, he produces out of thin air: a chop, potatoes, peas. GRACE fetches him a newspaper as he produces a napkin from thin air which he tucks into his shirt.

He pours wine from his newspaper into the glass.
GRACE takes the dove from the cage as if it is alive. She
fastens it to her finger, pets it.
He starts his dinner.
GRACE swings the dove round her head on a string – as
though it is flying.)

MAGICIAN: This chop is cold.

GRACE: Of course it'll be cold if you insist on carrying it around up your sleeve all day.

MAGICIAN: Will you stop playing with that bloody dove for one minute?

GRACE: Someone has to give it some exercise.

(*He catches the dove out of the air. Will he kill it? He shoves*
the dove to GRACE who puts it back in the cage as he picks
up his cloak and exits through the wardrobe.
GRACE presents the slammed door, smiling. As she speaks,
she flaps the table up – contents and all.
As it flaps up, the duvet comes out of another cupboard.
GRACE folds the chair and passes it out of a cupboard, then
takes off the leotard she speaks.)

I remember the night we met.

He produced assorted toffees from behind my ears and the rest of the world seemed to melt away.

I thought I'd cut the pack and turned up the Ace of Hearts. I wanted to have his children.

Maybe he's the six of spades. Five. The five of hearts.

I could take a gamble. I could put him back in the pack and I could get an eight of diamonds or a nine.

Or I might get the two of clubs.

I'll sleep on it.

(*She gets into bed.*)

Shuffle the pack tomorrow.

(*She is just about to fall asleep when CHIP's musical theme*
begins. He pulls back the duvet to reveal himself in bed with her.
GRACE screams.
He gets up and stands sideways on and turns his head to face
front, runs his hands up either side of his package, then puts
his hands on his waist.)

GRACE: Look, I – this is very flattering but...

(*As she continues, he runs his hands through his hair then, hands behind his head, flicks his head back and opens his arms wide, thrusting his groin forward.*)

I've really got to get eight hours sleep or I'll be good for nothing in the morning.

(*He takes one shoulder out of his jacket.*)

Well six. Six hours min.

(*Both shoulders. As she continues, he takes his jacket off.*)

I used to be able to go out, get pissed, get stoned, eat fifteen bags of crisps and shag all night and arrive at work looking better than ever.

(*He circles his hips up and down.*)

CHIP: (*Sings.*) I am the key to your door.

I'll take you places you've only dreamt of before.

GRACE: Now I can't even remember where my office is.

CHIP: (*Sings.*) Let me in.

Let go.

Let's go.

Unlock yourself.

(*He points at her and licks his lips.*)

GRACE: By ten o'clock at night, I'm not really interested in sex.

(*With his back to the audience, he bounces with his hands on his knees, then looks through his legs.*)

I haven't got the energy.

(*As she continues, he removes his waistcoat to reveal collar and cuffs – no shirt.*)

And there's so much else I should be doing.

I get to the end of the day and my list of things to do is longer than when I started.

(*He shakes a leg, shakes it again, then holds it out, then steps forward throwing his head back.*)

There was so much I was going to do today and I haven't even thought of half of it.

(*He links his hands above his head and does groin thrusts.*)

CHIP: (*Sings.*) You've waited such a long time for me to call.

I've seen the front door, now show me the hall.

GRACE: I haven't stopped. I haven't had lunch. I haven't done any paperwork.

CHIP: (*Sings.*) Open up and let me in.
    Knock knock.
    Let's go.
    Unlock yourself.
    (*He runs his hand through his hair, down his chest, to the waistband of his trousers.*)
GRACE: Well…
    (*He undoes his top trouser button.*)
    No.
    (*He undoes all his trouser buttons*)
    I can't.
    (*He punches the air – to one side then the other.*)
    I was, well…
    (*He puts his hands on his hips, circles his hips.*)
    What I'd really like to do is –
    (*He rips his trousers off.*)
    No I can't.
    (*He tweaks his bow tie.*)
    I'm embarrassed.
    (*He walks towards her.*)
    It's just, I have this real urge –
    (*He touches her under her chin.*)
    To –
    (*He moves closer.*)
    Have –
    (*He gets into bed.*)
    A baby.
    (*He moves away from her, pulling the duvet over him as she tries to caress him.*)
    We don't have to.
    It was only an idea.
    We don't have to if you don't want to.
    We can just cuddle up together.
    I wouldn't do anything you didn't want to.
    (*The duvet has flattened out – CHIP has gone.*)
    Chip. Chip! Chip!
    (*She pulls back the duvet he's gone.*)
    Shit.
    (*She lies down.*)

Go to sleep.
(*The clock music begins. She sits up.*)
Idiot.
(*Gets up.*)
Calm down.
(*Sits on the bed. The music builds.*)
What did you say that for?
I can't sleep.
Stupid cow.
Tidy room.
(*The BIRD pops out of the clock, mimicking her like a parrot.*)
BIRD: Tidy room.
GRACE: Hoover.
BIRD: Hoover.
GRACE: Get fit.
BIRD: Get fit.
GRACE: Phone Mum.
BIRD: Phone Mum.
GRACE: Stop!
(*The BIRD goes as she pulls the duvet off the bed and wraps it around her – revealing the bath. She paces around.*)
Set video.
(*The BIRD pops out again.*)
BIRD: (*Whispers.*) Video.
GRACE: Get married. Pay Visa bill.
BIRD: Bill.
(*GRACE glares at the BIRD. It goes.*)
GRACE: Relax.
(*She notices the bath. Looks at it. Looks into it. Puts a toe in, gingerly. Twinkly music.*)
Have a bath.
(*She sheds the duvet. Music like a Radox advert begins. She gets in, relaxes. Blows bubbles.*
A CENTAUR enters with sheaves of papers, gives them to her.
The Radox music stops.)
GRACE: Do you mind, I'm just having a –
(*He exits.*

She gets out of the bath and puts the sodden papers on a shelf.
The music begins again and she gets back into the bath and
relaxes.
She scrubs her back.
The BIRD pops out of a cupboard with a moblie phone.
The music stops.)
GRACE: I'm just –
BIRD: Urgent call.
GRACE: Tell them I'll call back.
BIRD: Urgent.
(*She gets out of the bath and takes the phone.*
The BIRD goes.)
GRACE:Hello?
Yes it is.
I'm in the bath, actually.
Yes.
(*CENTAUR ONE leans out of a cupboard with piles of*
papers. She goes to him.)
CENTAUR ONE: Your signature –
GRACE: (*On the phone.*) Yes.
(*CENTAUR TWO leans out of another cupboard with sheaves*
of papers.)
CENTAUR ONE: Here, here and –
GRACE: (*On the phone.*) Yes.
CENTAUR TWO: For your attention.
GRACE: (*On the phone.*) Yes.
CENTAUR ONE: Date.
GRACE: (*On the phone.*) As soon as I get out.
CENTAUR TWO: Very important, very important –
(*He gives her papers as he speaks, which GRACE puts on the*
shelf.)
CENTAUR ONE: Here.
(*He goes.*)
CENTAUR TWO: Red alert.
(*He goes.*)
GRACE: (*On the phone.*) First thing I do.
(*She ends the phone call and puts one last piece of paper on*
the shelf. The shelf collapses. She turns to the bath. The phone
rings: she answers it.)

31

(*On the phone.*) My bubbles! My bubbles are bursting!
(*She gets back into the bath: the Radox theme plays, fast. She submerges the phone. Relaxes.*
A knock at a cupboard.
She ignores it.
Another knock.)
DIY MAN: Hello?
GRACE: Hello?
DIY MAN: (*Inside a cupboard.*) Hello?
GRACE: Who is it?
DIY MAN: Hello?
GRACE: I'm in the bath.
DIY MAN: Hello?
GRACE: Yes?
DIY MAN: Hello?
GRACE: What do you want?
DIY MAN: Hello?
GRACE: Could you come back later?
(*A moment. Then another knock.*
GRACE jumps out of the bath, puts her dressing gown on and goes to the cupboard. She opens it – it's a very small cupboard.
The DIY MAN squeezes himself out of it and into the room – with some power tools. He examines the cupboard fastening as he enters.)
DIY MAN: The lock stile's binding against the frame – hinge recess is too deep.
GRACE: Do you want a drink?
(*GRACE shoves the duvet out through the cupboard and shuts the door.*)
DIY MAN: Don't mind if I do.
GRACE: Tea? Coffee? Wine?
DIY MAN: Never say no to a cup of tea.
GRACE: I suppose you meet a lot of women.
(*The DIY MAN sees the shelf.*)
DIY MAN: Ooh – hello.
GRACE: In your line of work. In their homes.
DIY MAN: I'll have to replace your flat heads, bridge the wall studs with a cross member fastened with a coach screw.

GRACE: I suppose most of them are dressed.

DIY MAN: Five sixteenths by two is ten sixteenths minus two is eight gauge. I'll have to locate the studs.

GRACE: I suppose most of them brush their hair.

(*He taps the wall.*)

I suppose they feel things less deeply. Laugh more –

(*She laughs.*)

Cry less.

(*She cries.*)

I suppose they don't shout: (*She shouts.*) 'Help me – I'm drowning!' or: 'Please catch me!'

(*She falls – like a plank of wood. Without stopping talking, he catches her and props her up against a wall – like a plank of wood.*)

DIY MAN: I'd go for a laddered frame – or bridging system with fixed batons, but your wall's throwing it out of square – unless it was packed or scribed. If it was an alcove, a lipped shelf with batten supports – or cross battens on a stud partition.

GRACE: Help!

(*She runs around the space.*)

Somebody help!

Somebody!

DIY MAN: An adjustable system with two dowels plugged through the wall battens – one through the end panel and the other engaging a batten fixed under the shelf, with the battens and shelves in hemlock, the ends in birch plywood, ramin dowels.

(*A door opens, revealing a DOCTOR in a waxed jacket. He has a Landrover Discovery door. He leans over it. His theme tune plays. He poses for a moment, then enters with the door, like a briefcase. He puts it down and catches GRACE as she falls.*)

DIY MAN: I wouldn't rule out lap-jointing the long rails to the end rails, glueing and pinning the cross rails and rub-joint triangular blocks – mounting the whole thing.

DOCTOR: When was your last period?

GRACE: I'm trying as hard as I can. I can't do this. I can't hold down a career. I can't even have a bath.

(*The DIY MAN EXAMINES THE ALCOVE.*)

DIY MAN: Bit of a shake on this.

(*The DOCTOR lets go of GRACE, who starts to fall. He goes to his car door, winds the window up and locks the door. As he continues, the DIY MAN catches her and drags her to the wall.*)

Your twenty-inch length really needs to be five-eighths – or a half-inch on blockboard.

DOCTOR: Do you think you might be pregnant?

(*As he continues, the DIY MAN nails GRACE to the wall.*)

DIY MAN: I could chamfer off the waste, round off the top front corners to a quarter-inch radius.

GRACE: It's all right for you with your healing the sick, heritage Britain life. You've got what you want.

(*GRACE tries to get away from the wall.*)

What about what I want?

(*The DOCTOR returns.*)

DIY MAN: You want to wipe these with methylated spirits, set it alight and burnish with wax. Build up the surface and finish with a rubber, flow the final coat into the surrounding surface.

DOCTOR: Might you be pregnant?

(*GRACE battles to get away from the wall as the DOCTOR takes a sweet from his pocket, eats it.*

He goes to the car door, unlocks it and puts the sweet wrapper in the rubbish container. Locks the car door.)

GRACE: It's not that. It's desire. It's passion. I want – I really, really want –

DIY MAN: You really want matt laminate on blockboard, with the core running the length of the shelf. You'd need a backing veneer to counter the pull, and a flexible edging strip or aluminium edging mitred at the corners.

DOCTOR: Why don't you make an appointment at the family planning clinic? Have a chat to the nurse.

(*The DIY MAN finishes the shelf.*)

DIY MAN: That's fixed that then, love.

(*The DIY MAN opens the cupboard door.*)

GRACE: I'll tell you what I want, what I really, really want?

(*The DOCTOR goes to fetch his car door.*)

DOCTOR / DIY MAN: So tell me what you want, what
you really, really want –
(*The DIY MAN tries to squeeze into the cupboard.*)
GRACE: I wanna –
(*The DOCTOR whacks her round the head with his door.*)
Ha!
(*She reels.*)
DIY MAN: Could you just give me a little shove?
(*She collapses.*

*The DOCTOR gives the part of his door that hit her a rub
with a chamois cloth.*)
Not to worry.
Night, love.
(*He goes.*

*The DOCTOR adjusts his wing mirror – his theme plays –
and he exits with his door.*

A moment.

GRACE starts to come round.)
GRACE: What am I doing down here?
(*DARCY pops up in the bath – his theme plays.*)
I'm soaking wet.
(*DARCY shakes the water from his head.*)
Bath.
(*She starts to get up.*)
I was in the…(bath).
(*DARCY gets out of the bath.*)
Can I get you a drink?
(*He stares at her.*)
Tea? Coffee? Wine?
Tea.
I was making some tea.
(*He stares.*)
Why do you keep staring at me?
I love your brooding silence but we can't carry on like
this. I need to know: When you close your eyes, do you
see me? Do we share the same dreams?
(*He rides back out through the wardrobe.*)
Tell me! Tell me.

(The clock music begins.
GRACE is ready for the BIRD to appear. She finds something
to whack it with and waits by the clock. It opens – a BABY
puppet peeps out.
GRACE just stops herself from whacking it and takes it.)
I want you. So much. Your little eyes looking up at me
are the whole world. I yearn for you. But I can't possibly
get pregnant. I've got too much to do. I've put
everything into this career for the last eight years. I can't
just stop. And I haven't met your father yet. I'm sure if
we did meet we'd fall in love at first sight and go on a
honeymoon to the Caribbean where you would be
conceived and we would love you so much. Having you
would be the happiest day of my life.
(A CENTURION puts his head through a door.)
CENTURION : Mark Anthony returns.
GRACE: Oh you are joking.
(He goes. She jumps up, changes into her Cleopatra gown
which is now in the wardrobe. She tidies round. As the bugle
sounds she remembers the baby – and shoves it in the freezer
compartment of the fridge. She opens the wardrobe to put the
pyjamas away – revealing a dejected looking MARK
ANTHONY.)
Can I get you a drink?
(He undoes his sword belt and throws it down.)
MARK: I lost twenty thousand men trying to conquer
Phaaspra.
GRACE: Tea? Coffee? Wine?
MARK: And another eight thousand on the way home.
GRACE: Sounds like you need a sit down.
MARK: I lost.
GRACE: Oh Mark.
MARK: It's over. I'm finished.
GRACE: You don't have to kill people to impress me.
MARK: Killing's all I know.
GRACE: You can make a new start.
MARK: The thunder of hooves.
GRACE: I'll help you with your CV.

MARK: The clash of steel on steel.

GRACE: You've got a very impressive CV.

MARK: The thud of steel on flesh.

GRACE: You're young, bright – clever, drop dead gorgeous.

MARK: I won't be special any more.

GRACE: Mark, you're very special.

MARK: I was important.

GRACE: You deserve a break.

MARK: I had an Empire.

GRACE: Be nice to yourself.

(*GRACE puts her earrings on him.*)

MARK: Men quaked when I walked into the room.

GRACE: Chill out.

MARK: Nations whispered my name.

GRACE: Spend some time at home.

MARK: I had everything and now I have nothing.

GRACE: We've got each other.

MARK: What am I going to do?

GRACE: You could get dinner – I won't be back until eight.

MARK: Grace –

(*She gets the bird cage.*)

GRACE: I'm sorry, Mark, but one of us has to earn some money.

(*She goes.*

He is left wearing the earrings. He feels them. Shakes his head a little. He likes them. He picks up her dress. Holds it up to himself.

The MAGICIAN's music begins.

The wardrobe door opens to reveal the MAGICIAN and GRACE. They come out onto the stage as MARK ANTHONY leaves.

GRACE smiles.

The MAGICIAN takes off his cloak, hat and gloves –she takes them. She brings on a guillotine. Presents it. He gestures for GRACE to get in. She gestures: me?

He gestures for her to step in.

She gestures: no.

He gestures for her to get in.

She does.

He gets a chainsaw from a cupboard. He laughs. He cuts her into two. He bows.

As GRACE continues, he does another trick: making the Ace of Hearts appear from a pack of cards.)

What about me?

Aren't you going to put me back together?

That's the best part of the trick.

(*He ignores her.*)

Get me out of here!

Put me back together!

I hate you!

(*He is going to leave. The MAGICIAN's music becomes the clock music.*)

You can't leave me like this.

You bastard.

I'm in pieces.

(*He leaves.*

GRACE battles with the guillotine.)

Why did you do this to me?

How am I supposed to live?

All I ever did was love you.

(*She gets up – still wearing the guillotine. She tries to walk to a cupboard – her feet go one way, her head the other. As she tries to master walking, the BIRD pops out of the clock – as Humphrey Bogart.*)

BIRD: You start your life with a deck of cards. You pick your first card – it's the Ace of Hearts. And you think you're going to be lucky all your life. Next you pick the six of spades. You're disappointed.

(*As GRACE speaks, the BIRD goes back into the clock and reappears with a needle and thread.*)

GRACE: At least it wasn't the five of clubs or the three of diamonds.

(*The BIRD gives the needle and thread to GRACE who starts to sew herself up – using the cloth from the trick to mop up the blood. She removes the guillotine and takes off the spangly leotard.*)

BIRD: So you hang onto it, wondering whether to spend the rest of your life with the six of spades or gamble for the Ace of Hearts. After a couple of years you decide to gamble. You pick a card. Kid yourself. Keep it face down and say: this is the one, this is my Ace of Hearts. Hoey: it's the two of clubs. You've got to put him back. You've lost your nerve, right sweetheart?

GRACE: It's just – the pack's looking a bit thin and I've got this terrible fear that if I put him back I'll end up with no card at all.

BIRD: Are you saying you're getting old?

GRACE: I'm not getting old, I just need to run an iron over my face.

(*She finishes sewing.*)

BIRD: Put him back in the pack, angel.

GRACE: I'm not feeling old or anything, I just want to leave my breasts in the fridge overnight to set. I'm fine.

(*She gives the BIRD the leotard, it takes it into the clock.*)

Single and fine.

Lots of very happy people are very single.

Happy and single and fine.

(*The BIRD reappears.*)

BIRD: Listen, precious –

(*GRACE stabs the BIRD with the needle, it disappears back into the clock.*)

GRACE: I don't want to be a single person. They're always the first to arrive and the last to leave and they drink too much and go on and on about the minutiae of their lives because they don't have anyone else to talk to or anyone else to think about and they always want to tell you – in medical detail – all about their last sexual encounter, which was seven months ago. I want to be one of a couple. Couples are great coz you get to team up with other couples and be double couples and go out with your mate and her guy and your guy, and he cracks jokes and enters into political debate and you sit there, so proud, and you turn to your mate and you give each other this: isn't he great? look. He's so funny and clever and – yours too. Thank you! Aren't they great? They can talk about a federal Europe, the relative values of the Mondeo and the Renault Laguna and impersonate Jimmy Saville, all on one pint of draft Bass.

(*As she continues, she opens a cupboard to reveal DARCY on his horse. His theme tune plays. He enters. Bows.*)

DARCY: Excuse me – your parents are in good health?

GRACE: They're fine. Can I get you a drink?

(*She is eager, always smiling at him.*)

DARCY: And all your sisters?

GRACE: I don't have any sisters. Tea? Coffee? Wine?

(*She straightens her bedraggled hair.*)

DARCY: And your parents are in good health?

GRACE: They're fine – well, if my mum knew you were here and I hadn't brushed my hair she'd go mad – I mean they'd section her – but they're fine, yes.

(*She sits down.*

He sits down.

They look at each other.)

DARCY: And your parents are in good health?

GRACE: They think I should wear more make-up. Rouge. I keep telling them, when I find my cheekbones I'll put some rouge on them. Mum's convinced that's why I haven't found a man and settled down. Got married. Rouge.

(*GRACE gets up, so DARCY gets up.*)

And dirty nails. And my body.

(*GRACE sits down, DARCY sits down.*)

My mother's got very big breasts.

(*They don't look at each other.*)

DARCY: And your family's in good health?

GRACE: I'm happy the way I am. This is what I tell them. I'm happy. Healthy. Fit.

(*She gets up and runs on the spot – so he gets up. As she continues her speech, she does the things she describes. Whenever it looks like she might sit down, DARCY goes to sit down too.*)

I do a lot of sport. Running. On the spot and off the spot. Weights. Tai chi. Well. I'm going to do a lot of sport. When I find the right gym.

(*They look at each other.*)
I've been meaning to get dressed.
I'll get dressed.
DARCY: Excuse me –
GRACE: It won't take a minute.
(*He bows and leaves, the door closes behind him.*)
(*After him.*) If you like me in my pyjamas you'll love me in –
(*She opens the wardrobe door – the DOCTOR is there with his Landrover Discovery door. His theme tune plays. He enters.*)
Would you like a drink?
DOCTOR: I'd love one.
GRACE: Tea? Coffee? Wine?
DOCTOR: Whisky.
(*She goes to the drinks cupboard, opens it. Inside is a whisky bottle and two tumblers. She pours two glasses.*)
I've had a hell of a day.
GRACE: You're not on call tonight, are you?
DOCTOR: Of course.
(*She gives one glass to the DOCTOR. She is very thirsty and downs her own.*)
Have we got any ice?
GRACE: Try the freezer.
(*He goes to the freezer.*)
DOCTOR: I'm going to have to go to the garage tomorrow as well. The rubbish container on the inside of my door is stuck.
GRACE: Is it?
DOCTOR: It's full of sweet wrappers.
(*He opens the freezer compartment and pulls out the BABY. It is blue.*)
What's this doing in here?
GRACE: What?
DOCTOR: The baby.
GRACE: Is it all right?
DOCTOR: It's frozen.
GRACE: Did you find the ice?
DOCTOR: We must be out.

GRACE: Will it thaw, do you think?

DOCTOR: How should I know?

GRACE: Wrap it in a blanket or something.

DOCTOR: How did it get in there?

GRACE: I was tidying round.

(*He looks at her.*)

I had to go to work and there was no-one to look after it.

I thought it said –

I thought it said somewhere: 'Suitable for home freezing.'

DOCTOR: Where?

GRACE: I thought it did.

DOCTOR: We never freeze them.

GRACE: It should have knocked.

DOCTOR: Never freeze babies.

GRACE: It should have knocked if it was cold.

(*He knocks it on the fridge – it's solid.*)

Can't you do something?

DOCTOR: Oh I don't know, Grace.

GRACE: You're a doctor.

DOCTOR: This isn't a common cold.

GRACE: I was just so busy.

I must have forgotten it was in there.

DOCTOR: What sort of a mother are you?

GRACE: It's a simple mistake.

It Scould've happened to anyone.

(*His bleeper goes. He starts to leave with his car door. Gives GRACE the BABY.*)

It'll thaw out.

I'll have it thawed out by the time you get back.

(*He leaves.*

She breathes on the BABY to try to defrost it. She opens a cupboard to get a blanket. Inside, a CENTAUR is on the toilet reading Motor Mart.)

Oh. Sorry.

(*She shuts the door. She hugs the BABY to her to try and warm it up.*)

I'm just a bit tired.

(*The BIRD pops out.*)

BIRD: You're overtired.

GRACE: I'm not overtired.

BIRD: You're snappy and overtired.

(*The DIY MAN knocks from the inside of a cupboard.*)

DIY MAN: Hello?

GRACE: Just – find a blanket.

DIY MAN: Hello?

(*She goes to another cupboard, looking for a blanket – the BABY is very cold. It is making her cold.*)

GRACE: Find a man.

(*The CENTURION pops his head out of his cupboard.*)

CENTURION: My Lord –

GRACE: Not now.

(*She slams the door on him.*

The BABY is so cold, she has to put it down.

She flaps down the flap-down table. She's about to put the BABY onto it when the MAGICIAN's hands appear and do a card trick: making the two of clubs appear from a pack.)

I knew it.

(*She closes the table flap.*)

MAGICIAN: (*Off.*) My hands!

GRACE: I'm sick of this.

(*She opens another cupboard, inside CHIP leans back and pours baby oil over himself as he sings.*)

CHIP: Let me in. Let go. Let's go –

(*She gives him the BABY.*

He puts baby oil on it and it becomes an Athena moment.

GRACE shuts the cupboard.)

GRACE: Get out – go on.

(*The BIRD pops out again, as Terry Thomas.*)

BIRD: Ding dong!

GRACE: I'm thirty tomorrow.

BIRD: Oh, hard cheese.

(*The BIRD laughs more and more maniacally.*)

Get away from me.

(*The BIRD goes as another cupboard opens to reveal the DOCTOR – he looks out of the cupboard as if it's his car door.*)

What are you looking at?

(*She storms off stage. As the DOCTOR closes his door, a door opens and DARCY rushes in.*)

DARCY: I –

(*He realises she isn't there.*)

Oh.

(*He goes. As he leaves, another cupboard opens and a CENTAUR enters. He sees the Ace of Hearts card lying on the floor. he picks it up, looks at it.*

GRACE pops her head out of a cupboard.)

GRACE: This is my life.

Just mine.

Just my life.

Not his.

Not ours.

My life.

It's my life.

(*GRACE slams her cupboard doors.*

As the CENTAUR goes, the introduction to 'It's My Life' begins. As we hit the chorus, a small, white DOG pokes its head out of a cupboard to do the backing vocals, and the wardrobe doors open to reveal GRACE in a white skirt and skates.

As they sing, GRACE skates out across the stage, doing twirls and jumps.)

DOG: It's my life!

GRACE: It's my life, my worries.

DOG: It's my life!

GRACE: It's my life, my problems.

(*The DOG goes as DARCY rushes in on his horse.*

He bows, rushes across the space, looks at the wall, turns to look at GRACE. Turns away, looks at her again. He walks past her, she twirls round each time he passes her. He walks away from her. Then towards her.

The DOG pops out again.)

DOG: It's my life!

GRACE: It's my life, my worries.

DOG: It's my life!

(*By now she is more interested in him than the song.*)

GRACE: It's my life, my…

(*She trails off and we return to the instrumental.*
GRACE keeps on the move throughout.)

DARCY: In vain I have suffered.

It will not do.

My feelings will not be repressed.

GRACE: I'm sorry I –

(*She indicates she has to go.*)

DARCY: You must allow me to tell you how ardently I admire and love you.

GRACE: Me?

DARCY: In declaring myself thus I am fully aware that I will be going expressly against the wishes of my family, my friends, and I hardly need add my own better judgement. But it cannot be helped.

(*As he speaks, she spins around him, trying to escape.*)

GRACE: Oh. I see. Oh no. Not now. No. No. You see – You don't understand, Mr Darcy.

Things have changed.

I've changed.

(*We build to the chorus as GRACE sings.*)

U-o-o-oh!

(*The chorus kicks in again: the DOG appears on top of the wardrobe, this time with the BIRD.*
They sing, GRACE speaks.)

DOG / BIRD: It's my life.

GRACE: My skirt is so white.

DOG / BIRD: It's my life!

GRACE: My legs are so smooth.

DOG / BIRD: It's my life.

GRACE: My face is so radiant.

DOG / BIRD: It's my life!

GRACE: My skates are so fast.

(*We return to the instrumental, the DOG and BIRD disappear.*)

DARCY: Almost from the earliest moments of our acquaintance I have come to feel for you a passionate admiration and regard which despite all my struggles has overcome every rational objection –

GRACE: Please don't. I can't. Oh please. Please.

I want to.

I do.

I have to go skating.

DARCY: I beg you most fervently to relieve me of my suffering.

(*The DOG appears out of a cupboard near GRACE – then goes.*)

GRACE: With my little white dog running alongside.

DARCY: Consent to be my wife.

(*A clock strikes eleven – a cupboard opens to reveal the BIRD banging a gong.*)

GRACE: Is that the time?

(*The BIRD goes.*)

DARCY: Is this all the reply I am to expect?

GRACE: Do you want me to die of Toxic Shock Syndrome?

(*She skates off.*

DARCY leans on a cupboard – his head on one forearm. He is disturbed. He walks to the front of the space. He turns, walks to the wardrobe, opens the wardrobe door to exit.

MARK ANTHONY enters through it – wearing full Cleopatra drag.)

DARCY: I shall conquer this.

I shall.

(*MARK ANTHONY decks him and he reels backwards into the wardrobe.*

MARK ANTHONY shuts the door.

A telephone rings.

MARK opens a cupboard door and takes out a mobile phone. He answers it.)

MARK: Marcus Anthonius.

(*As he talks, he gets a TV remote control from another cupboard and channel hops – Neighbours, racing, a film, a children's programme. He also preens himself in a mirror.*)

Lepidus. Hi.

Not bad.

Crap. Absolute crap.

I had to turn off in the end. I couldn't watch.

Gordon Strachan (*Or other appropriate football team manager.*) wants to run a broad sword through the lot of them.

I don't know. I'm supposed to be going to Armenia.
Where are we now? Thursday? Tuesday. I've got my
word-processing course.
I've got to. I haven't been for three weeks.
(*There is a banging from inside the wardrobe. He ignores it
and continues.*)
We've got to do a business plan.
I'll get Grace to do it.
She's at work.
I'm fine. I've drunk too much coffee.
I'm going into town.
I need a new doublet.
(*The banging gets louder.*)
I saw a lovely one. Open down the front with leather
straps across the chest and steel-capped shoulders.
Really smart.
Leather breeches.
I must get some exercise.
(*He goes to the wardrobe and opens the door. GRACE hangs
on a hanger, wearing the wedding dress, her feet dangling.
Without batting an eyelid – or stopping speaking – he reaches
in and lifts her down – dress, hanger and all.*)
Yeah – sparring would be good. Or a long march without
water.
(*As he continues his phone call, GRACE tries to undo the
dress. However, her arms stick out from her sides – she only
has use of her lower arms. She swings them, but they won't
reach the fastenings. She gets madder and madder.*)
Maybe at the end of the week.
(*GRACE stands, her arms swinging.*)
Okay Lep. Yeah.
Cheers.
(*He hangs up. A moment.*)
GRACE: What's for dinner?
MARK: Some work's come up with Lepidus. It's ninety-nine
  percent certain.
GRACE: Have you been shopping?
MARK: We've just got to finalise the details. I've got a
  really good feeling about it.

GRACE: What about the washing-up?

(*He wiggles his fingers at her.*)

MARK: I couldn't find my Marigolds.

(*He helps her take the dress off.*)

GRACE: Some conqueror you've turned out to be.

MARK: This isn't my forte.

GRACE: And what is?

Killing people with swords and travelling the world in a galleon? Society has moved on a little in the last two and a half thousand years.

(*He finishes taking the wedding dress off her.*)

What are you going to do about it?

MARK: Oh I'm sick as a pig about the whole thing.

GRACE: I get up at six-thirty, go to work, go to Tesco's in my lunch hour, come home, put the dinner on, tidy round, wash up.

I'd rather be dead than living like this.

MARK: Me too.

GRACE: It's a living/hell.

MARK: Hell.

GRACE: I'd rather kill myself.

MARK: If you kill yourself, I'll kill myself.

(*He goes to leave.*)

GRACE: Where are you going?

MARK: I'm going to get out of this dress. I can't begin to think about money unless I feel a million dollars, and this makes me feel about fourteen ninety-nine.

(*He shuts the cupboard door behind him.*

GRACE goes to the wardrobe for something to wear, opens it. Inside are two tiny plastic lunch cases, two tiny coats on hangers and two tiny pairs of shoes.)

GRACE: Cleo!

(*She takes out the lunch cases, puts them on the floor.*)

Alex!

Who's got swimming this morning?

Come on!

(*She takes out a tiny coat and holds it low to the ground – waiting for a child to enter and put it on.*)

We're going to be late.

Now remember, Daddy's picking you up today, but I'll be back in time to read you a story.

(*She goes to the wardrobe.*)

Where are you?

(*She puts the coat and sandwich cases back in and the doors shut.*)

You're not in here.

(*She looks for them.*)

Where are you hiding?

(*She opens another cupboard – nothing.*)

I know. I know where you are.

(*Opens another cupboard – nothing.*)

I can't find you.

Come out, come out wherever you are.

We're going to be late.

I'm not playing now, I'm being serious.

(*She opens the wardrobe – the cases, coats and shoes have gone.*)

No.

(*She searches the wardrobe.*)

I thought –

Children, children, children, children….

Didn't I…

(*She touches her belly. Ticking builds throughout.*)

Oh no!

It completely slipped my mind. I completely forgot.

I've forgotten to have them. I've forgotten to have the children. What was I thinking? Too complicated. Too many heads. It was just – I was just so busy and –

(*She knocks on the clock door.*)

Where's the button?

(*The BIRD comes out – she grabs it.*)

Where's the rewind button?

(*The BIRD exclaims and tries to escape as she throttles/manhandles it.*)

Quick, quick –

(*As the BIRD gasps for breath, we hear the clock start to speed up.*)

49

It's not too late. I just need a bit more –
(*The clock goes mad – hands spinning round, BIRD writhing – then everything stops dead on midnight. The BIRD is dead.*)
No! No!
(*MARK knocks from inside his cupboard.*)
MARK: Let me in.
GRACE: No! Please!
MARK: I know you love me.
GRACE: Oh God.
   (*MARK continues, we hear knocking in another cupboard.*)
DIY MAN: (*Inside the cupboard.*) Hello?
MARK: Help me.
DIY MAN: Hello?
MARK: Help!
DIY MAN: Hello?
MARK: Please!
DIY MAN: Anyone at home?
   (*GRACE opens the second door and the DIY MAN comes out. The playing card the Ace of Hearts sticks out of the top pocket of his boiler suit.*
   He goes over to the biological clock.)
GRACE: Please don't touch that.
DIY MAN: I don't know if I can do anything with it.
GRACE: It was working a minute ago.
   (*MARK ANTHONY bangs.*)
DIY MAN: Is there someone in the cupboard?
GRACE: No.
DIY MAN: I can hear knocking.
GRACE: It's the central heating.
DIY MAN: Have you got any thermostatic valves?
GRACE: I don't know.
   (*He starts to take her biological clock apart.*)
DIY MAN: If you're lucky, it's just friction wear on the
   pivots, or pinions – could be the pallets.
   Might need replacing.
   (*GRACE notices the playing card.*)
   You'll be in trouble if it's the fusee chain.
   (*He takes the workings out.*)

You've had this a while. When did you last clean it?
Should be cleaned every two years. Look at all the dirt
in the movement.
(*She looks intently at the playing card.*)
That's dust and atmospheric impurities combined with
the oil on the moving parts. Quite an abrasive mixture.
(*She reaches for the playing card – he looks at her – she
stops.*)
GRACE: Can I get you a drink?
DIY MAN: Shouldn't have let it get dusty.
GRACE: Tea? Coffee? Wine?
DIY MAN: I never drink with thirty-year-old women –
they're always weighing you up as father material.
Your recoil escapement's corroded. Look at that.
Damp's caused that.
Neglect will always destroy a clock.
(*GRACE reaches for the card again – he looks.*)
GRACE: Excuse me – is that the Ace of Hearts in your
pocket?
DIY MAN: What?
GRACE: Do you mind if I –
(*She pulls the card out – another follows, and another, and
another…and so on. She keeps pulling.*)
GRACE: One, two, three, four five, six, seven –
DIY MAN: Here – what are you playing at?
GRACE: I'm sorry, I thought – nineteen, twenty, twenty-
one –
DIY MAN: Where's all that lot coming from?
GRACE: Just hold still a minute. Thirty-three, thirty-four –
DIY MAN: I don't like the look of this thirty-eight, thirty-
nine –
GRACE: I didn't realise there'd been so many.
DIY MAN: Forty-three, forty-four, forty-five, forty-six,
forty-seven, forty-eight –
GRACE: So much time.
So much water.
So much I thought I'd have done.
My life, my life.
DIY MAN: / Forty-nine, fifty, fifty-one –

(*The last card pops out – the two of clubs.*)
Fifty-two.

GRACE: There's so much to do.

DIY MAN: Says who?

GRACE: What?

DIY MAN: Says who?

(*MARK ANTHONY knocks again.*)

MARK: I love you.

(*The DIY MAN looks at her.*)

I'm in hell.

GRACE: I haven't got time for all this.

MARK: I need you.

Let me in!

DIY MAN: I think there is someone in your cupboard.

MARK: Please let me in.

(*The DIY MAN packs his tools up, leaving the clock in pieces.*)

DIY MAN: I think he wants to come in.

MARK: I can't live without you.

DIY MAN: I'll go and have a word.

GRACE: Tell him I'm dead.

Tell him I've killed myself.

(*The DIY MAN opens the door to MARK ANTHONY, but blocks his entry into the room. GRACE hides.*)

DIY MAN: Can I help you at all?

MARK: I have to see her.

DIY MAN: She's dead.

MARK: How did she die?

DIY MAN: She killed herself.

MARK: Why?

(*The DIY MAN looks at GRACE.*)

GRACE: For his love.

DIY MAN: For your love.

(*MARK ANTHONY exits, shutting the cupboard door behind him.*

GRACE goes over to the clock, looks at all the different pieces.)

You want to kick him into touch.

(*A shout from off as MARK ANTHONY drives his sword into himself.*)

Get yourself a nice stereo and a set of headphones.

(*GRACE sits on the edge of the bed.*)

Or a little cat.

MARK: I die!

(*GRACE lies down.*)

DIY MAN: I love animals.

(*The cupboard door opens and MARK ANTHONY staggers in, his sword sticking out of him. GRACE quickly plays dead on the bed. As he speaks, he reels towards GRACE, ending up lying on her bed. He presumes she is dead.*

The DIY MAN watches.)

MARK: It is you who fill the rich earth and buoyant seas with your presence. It is through you that every living thing achieves its life. Goddess of ten thousand names, shelter and heaven to all mankind, the house of life, the word of God, the great Mother of All the Gods of Nature.

(*The DIY MAN whips across the stage and is about to open his cupboard when MARK ANTHONY begins again. He freezes.*

Likewise, GRACE thinks he is dead and rises to leave but he begins again – she lies down again.)

The whole of wisdom and philosophy, making our lives worth living, giving us strength to endure our days on earth, purifying our souls.

(*The DIY MAN opens his cupboard and gets in.*)

DIY MAN: Night love.

(*GRACE also thinks he is dead – goes to rise – but no.*)

MARK: The power of the sea, of the Nile, of the moon, of love and healing, of the underworld and life beyond the grave.

(*She rises – he is nearly dead.*)

I beg you not to grieve over this wretched change in my fortunes.

(*He dies.*

The CENTURION sticks his head out of a cupboard.)

CENTURION: My Lord – we are defeated. The troups are deserting –

Octavian is…

(*GRACE motions that MARK is dead.*)

Christ – no.

(*He goes.*

GRACE puts the duvet over MARK ANTHONY's body –
enabling him to secretly exit! GRACE rushes round the space.
She tries a cupboard door, it won't open. She tries all the
cupboard doors – none of them will open. Eventually, the
door of a small cupboard opens, she gets in and shuts the door
behind her as the CENTURION peeps out again.)

My lady – we are defeated. The troups are deserting –
Octavian is taking the city.

(*The stage is empty.*)

They are breaking down the barricades!

(*He goes.*

Music begins.

As the music builds, a wardrobe opens to reveal GRACE in
a swimming costume. She has goggles on her forehead. As she
speaks, the CENTAURS enter.)

I've got to do this now.

If I don't do it now I'll have to do it tomorrow and
tomorrow I'm thirty and I'll have to eat cake and smile.

(*The music builds a little. As she continues, she puts her*
goggles on and prepares to dive.)

I've got to do it while I'm still in my twenties. If I don't
do it while I'm still in my twenties I'll have to do it
when I'm in my thirties, and I've already got all the
other stuff I was going to do in my twenties to do in my
thirties.

I've got to do this.

(*As she says this last line, the music builds and she dives into*
the CENTAURS' arms.

Once she has landed, CENTAUR ONE begins.)

CENTAUR ONE: Tidy room.

Hoover.

Sort out washing.

Fix cupboard door.

Put up shelves.

Have a child.

Make some tea.

Get out of bed.

Buy: pasta, lettuce, cheese, olives, bread, Ultra Bra, baked beans, washing-up liquid.

Get up.

Get fit.

Learn Russian.

Decide what to wear.

CENTAUR TWO: Water. Cold. Thick. Salt stops the blood.

(*GRACE surfaces.*)

Slide.

(*She brings an arm forward to begin the crawl.*)

Slice.

(*The hand enters the water.*)

Slide.

(*The other arm moves forward.*)

GRACE: I've got to –

(*Instead of breathing, GRACE speaks each time she brings her head to the surface.*)

CENTAUR TWO: Slice.

(*That hand enters the water.*)

GRACE: I've got to –

CENTAUR TWO: Slide.

GRACE: Something I've got to do.

Something I must –

Remember.

To –

CENTAUR TWO: Losing sight of land.

Just a horizon.

Grey above.

CENTAUR ONE: Cut nails. Eat. Breathe.

CENTAUR TWO: Grey below. Slide. Slice. Breathe.

GRACE: Breathe.

(*She changes to breaststroke.*)

CENTAUR ONE: Phone Mum. Phone bank. Put wash on. Back up computer discs. Pay Visa bill.

Get married. Set video. Listen to classical music. Wash hair. Swim the channel.

Get into a steady relationship. Unload washing. Do lottery syndicate. Read reports. Find a man. Get promoted. Decide what to wear. Iron clothes. Paint skirting board.

CENTAUR TWO: Glide.

(*GRACE holds her arms out in front.*)

Sweep – breathe.

(*She makes the breast stroke.*)

Glide.

Sweep – breathe.

Wave.

(*A wave makes her bob up and down.*)

Another wave.

(*This time it engulfs her.*)

Covered in lard.

Stay afloat.

GRACE: Stay calm.

I've got to.

Not worry.

No time.

So cold.

So hungry.

Just want sleep.

If I could sleep.

Let go.

For a minute.

Can't.

Mustn't.

I must keep my head above water.

I can cope.

I am coping.

CENTAUR ONE: Bury Mark Anthony. Swim channel. Fix central heating. Buy Tampax. Feed dog.

(*She changes to doing the butterfly.*)

CENTAUR TWO: Thumbs down.

Head up.

Elbows out.

Thumbs down.

Head up.

Elbows out.

A wave.

(*It engulfs her.*)

GRACE: If I can just make it through today, I'll be fine.

(*She treads water.*)

If I can just get through this sentence, I'll –

CENTAUR ONE: Phone Mum. Kettle. Skirting board. Family. Husband. Milk bottles. Shelf. Reports. Tea. Baby. Man. Get. Find. Do. Paint. Listen. Make. Get. Have. Learn. Do. Do. Fetch.

CENTAUR TWO: Peddle. Peddle. Salt. Water. Salt.

(*She goes under – resurfaces.*)

GRACE: Going under.

(*She goes under again, fights her way up.*)

CENTAUR TWO: Peddle.

GRACE: Going under.

CENTAUR TWO: Peddle.

GRACE: What was on the list?

CENTAUR TWO: Salt.

GRACE: Where's the list?

CENTAUR TWO: Water.

GRACE: I won't let it get on top of me.

CENTAUR TWO: Salt. What. A. Into. Out. Up. Out.

GRACE: Help!

(*They hold her but she fights out of their grasp.*)

I don't need any help.

I'm sinking.

(*She starts to go down.*)

Help me! No!

I'm drowning.

Aaaagh!

(*She drowns, disappearing into the bed. They look. Then get the duvet. Place it over the hole. One exits while the other smoothes the duvet. The first enters again with a banner. They put it up across the wardrobe doors. It reads: Happy Birthday 30 Today. The first takes out a hooter. Blows it. A moment. They exit. The stage is empty. GRACE flings back the duvet and gets out of the bed, her back to the audience.*)

She is naked and dripping wet. She wears a dry paper party hat on her head. She walks to the wardrobe, opens the double doors and walks through them – breaking the banner. They close behind her.)

CAKE
from a collaboration with Jade

With special thanks to Janet Morgan, baker and cake artist at Jane Asher Party Cakes, London, for sharing her expertise, and Dr Iain Law at Birmingham University's Philosophy Department for helpful discussion.

Characters

MUM

JOHN

The rest of the cast are made up of inanimate objects, brought to life by two animators. They are as follows:

WOODEN SPOON

TEA SPOON

TABLE SPOON

LADLE

SPATULA

SHARP KNIFE

They are sometimes collectively referred to as
THE UTENSILS.

Cake was first performed at The Door, Birmingham Repertory Theatre on 25 September 2003, with the following cast:

MUM, Victoria Worsley

JOHN / ANIMATION, Steve Tiplady

ANIMATION, Rebekah Wild

Director, Emma Bernard

Designer, Delia Peel

Lighting Designer, Charles Balfour

Composer, Nigel Piper

Production Manager, Matthew Darby

Technical Manager, Marcia Stephenson

Scene 1

A long counter. At one end there is an operational sink and draining board, at the other there is a cooker with working oven and a working ring. There is a big shelf behind the counter on which are laid all the things to make a cake: mixing bowls, scales, ingredients, wooden spoons of different shapes and sizes, a whisk, a metal tablespoon, a wooden spatula and a tea-spoon. There is also a ladle. MUM is about to demonstrate how to make a cake to her audience. As she speaks, the two Animators lay the table with packets of all the required ingredients. They also lay out all the equipment she will need. MUM addresses the audience, imparting important information.

MUM: Victoria Sponge.
  For the cake you will need:
  175g of butter
  175g of caster sugar, eggs three – medium, and 175g of self raising flour.
  (*The Animators step back. Everything is ready. The cake-making is about to begin.*)
  For a Victoria Sponge you need the same amount of fat to sugar – so for a seven-inch cake, we're using 175g of sugar –
  (*She weighs it out and pours it into the bowl.*)
  And 175g of butter.
  (*As she does the same with the butter, the two Animators move slightly closer to her – active now, not just observers. They watch her with interest.*)
  Mix them together to a fluffy consistency – until it's the colour of cream.
  I'm using the back of a wooden spoon.
  (*She picks up WOODEN SPOON and begins to cream them together. The Animators may move closer to the counter.*)
  This is a sponge, as opposed to a Madeira – a Madeira you'd use for a wedding cake – any cake that needs to support a substantial amount of decoration. It's a firmer cake, the difference between a Madeira and a sponge being that extra ounce more flour to egg for the Madeira which gives it that firmer texture.

You can cream your butter and sugar for two minutes. I cream mine by sight, but you could cream for three, four – even five minutes. Five minutes is a maximum.

(*She puts the spoon down as she shows us the mixture. One of the animators moves to the WOODEN SPOON. Slowly it starts to stir (!). It rolls on one side to look at her. She looks for the WOODEN SPOON. It plays dead. She picks it up and beats the sugar and butter together with it.*)

You want the butter at room temperature, not straight out of the fridge – otherwise you'll be there all day.

(*She puts down WOODEN SPOON again to show us the mixture.*)

So remove the butter from the fridge an hour or two before it's needed.

(*Then she starts to prepare the eggs. Again WOODEN SPOON watches.*)

When the mixture is light and fluffy add three lightly beaten eggs – all you really need to do is to break the yolks, you don't need to whip it up. Break them into a separate bowl.

(*She breaks the eggs into a bowl – now WOODEN SPOON stands up. It pays real attention – this woman, as far as WOODEN SPOON is concerned, is a goddess.*

MUM picks up WOODEN SPOON to break the egg yolks.)

You can throw all the ingredients in together but that will give you a much denser sponge than doing it this way. A sponge is all about air – the whole point is to create a lovely light cake by incorporating as much air as possible.

(*MUM pours the eggs in to the mixture, putting down WOODEN SPOON.*)

And beat the eggs in.

Quite slowly. For one to two minutes.

(*She looks for WOODEN SPOON. Quick as a wink, it jumps into her hand. For MUM, this is completely normal.*)

Don't worry if the eggs curdle, just add some flour after you put in each egg.

Next you need 175g of flour.

(*MUM beats the eggs in, using WOODEN SPOON. Then*

she starts to organise the flour – leaving WOODEN SPOON
beating the eggs in by itself. First she cleans the scales.)
You can use self-raising flour, or you can use plain flour
with 25g of raising agent – baking powder. You can
make your own. Or just use self-raising flour if it's
simpler.
(*She looks over at WOODEN SPOON who is beating away.*)
Good.
(*As MUM continues, WOODEN SPOON gets more and more*
enthusiastic with its beating. MUM tries not to intervene.)
Sieving the flour will give you greater aeration.
(*The spoon keeps going, very enthusiastic.*)
Aeration gives sponge cake a lighter consistency.
(*She comes back over to WOODEN SPOON.*)
And – that'll do.
(*She halts WOODEN SPOON. WOODEN SPOON hops*
out of the bowl into a standing position – with mixture all
over its head like a hairstyle.)
Some people sieve the flour three or four times – which
will give you even more aeration.
(*MUM notices and wipes the mixture from its head.*)
Whoopsie.
(*As she continues, WOODEN SPOON jumps back into the*
bowl and starts beating again. MUM goes over to the oven.)
Anyone can follow a recipe. Anyone can give a cake a
mix and say: that'll do.
(*She pulls WOODEN SPOON out of the mixture again.*)
(*To WOODEN SPOON.*) That's enough.
(*WOODEN SPOON gets back in the bowl again.*)
If ten people follow the same recipe, you'll get ten
different cakes. It's all in the mixing.
(*She takes the spoon out of the mixture and whacks it on the*
side of the bowl without thinking, then stands it up. It is
concussed and staggers about – just as she's about to go to the
oven. She realises.)
I'm sorry.
(*She takes the TEA SPOON and scrapes the mixture off*
instead.)
All right?

(*WOODEN SPOON nods and she puts TEA SPOON down.
As she goes to the oven, WOODEN SPOON jumps back into
the bowl and starts to beat again.*)

Your oven needs to be preheated to gas mark 4 or 180
degrees.

I think that's enough beating. You can over-beat a mix
and it'll become too liquid.

(*TEA SPOON is watching WOODEN SPOON with great
admiration. MUM doesn't notice this as she takes WOODEN
SPOON out of the mixture and this time grabs the TABLE
SPOON to scrape the mixture off with. Again she goes to the
oven. This time when WOODEN SPOON jumps up and
begins to mix again, both TEA SPOON and the TABLE
SPOON are watching. The bowl is spinning wildly.*)

A hundred and eighty degrees.

If you overbeat, the cake will have no stability. It'll rise
– but then it'll completely collapse, giving you this M
fault.

(*She demonstrates the M fault with her hands.*)

Come out of there now.

(*WOODEN SPOON jumps out of the bowl.*)

Weigh out 175g of flour.

(*The flour is on the other end of the counter. As she looks
round for it, TEA SPOON and TABLE SPOON rush off to
help. They start to open the bag of flour. MUM hasn't noticed.*)

And you're going to fold the flour in, very slowly. If you
knock the air out of your cake at this point, it won't rise.

(*She moves the LADLE out of the way in order set up the
scales. The LADLE gets involved with the flour too and all of
them – ant-like – start to bring spoonfuls over. WOODEN
SPOON bangs its end on the counter excitedly.*)

Just a minute.

(*It bangs again to attract attention to the flour-carriers.*)

In a minute.

(*The scales are ready. As MUM continues, the carriers start
to arrive. They pour the flour in, then go back to fetch more.*)

Before you add the flour, scrape the bowl down.

(*She uses WOODEN SPOON to scrape the bowl down.*)

Butter will cling to the edge of the bowl and if there are

unmixed ingredients, they can disrupt the cake. You'd notice, after it's baked, white dots inside the cake and speckles on the crust.

(*MUM notices the penultimate utensil – TABLE SPOON – depositing its flour in the scales. It follows the first carriers back to the bag.*)

Perhaps a bloom of sugar. You want a nice, smooth top.

(*Meanwhile, LADLE deposits its load.*)

Thank you.

And no streaking running through the cake.

(*While she looks at how much there is, the snake of carriers begin to work its way over to her again – this time joined by a rather sticky WOODEN SPOON who can resist no longer. TABLE SPOON delivers its load first – and returns to the flour bag for more.*)

I think that's enough.

(*TEA SPOON deposits its load and returns to the flour bag.*)

Oh. Okay.

(*TABLE SPOON deposits its load.*)

That's enough.

(*LADLE wants to deposit its load.*)

That's enough –

(*She tries to stop LADLE – but LADLE is determined – and the others are returning now with more.*)

I don't need any more flour. That's enough flour. That's six hundred –

(*LADLE manages to deposit its load.*)

Six hundred grams. That's six hundred grams.

(*WOODEN SPOON is next – all sticky. While she talks to him – the others deposit more and more flour.*)

That's it. No more. Take it back. Go on. You're all sticky! That's no good. That's wasted – all that flour is wasted, isn't it? It's no good. Come here –

(*She takes it to the bin and empties its flour into the bin. This is very upsetting for it. It is still covered in cake mixture. She stands it on the worktop. She looks at the scales.*)

Eight hundred grams.

(*She stops the next carrier.*)

Enough flour. Put it back. Put it all back.

(*She turns him back. They all start to take the flour back while she measures out the right amount using WOODEN SPOON. By this point the snake of spoons are arriving with eggs.*)

No more eggs. We've done the eggs.

(*She takes the eggs from them – but they keep bringing her eggs – she can't hold any more. She starts giving them back until some are returning one, then picking up another – a cycle that she never seems able to get out of. Maybe occasionally she does get a hand free and is about to move on with the recipe, when more eggs appear. As she does so, she talks to us about eggs.*)

These are medium eggs. Make sure when you're following a recipe that you don't use large eggs instead of medium. If it doesn't specify, always go for medium. You don't want too much egg.

(*In the end, she grabs TEA SPOON by its throat.*)

No more eggs. Okay. We don't need any more eggs. That's it for eggs.

(*She lies him down. Puts the egg back on him and turns him round – pushes him across surface, fast – an Animator just catches him.*)

Sift the flour into the mixture in about four lots.

(*Defiant, TEA SPOON pushes the egg back to MUM who just catches it. They stare at each other, then TEA SPOON goes to his drawer. He gets in.*)

Don't use a whisk – that might be fine for a Génoise, not for a sponge.

(*Out of the drawer comes SPATULA. They all go over to MUM.*)

You can use a metal spoon. It's got a nice sharp edge, which will cut through the mix. Or you can use a beater. Not too hard – we don't want to spill any, do we?

(*This goes quite well. She sets up: SPATULA mixing. WOODEN SPOON tapping the sieve. LADLE joins in tapping the sieve. TABLE SPOON takes turns with SPATULA at folding the flour into the mixture.*)

And the important bit is that you're folding it in –

keeping lots of air in the mixture.

*(This all happens in relays: the tappers tap while the mixers
wait, then the mixers mix while the tappers wait. This repeats.
Music begins.)*

Everything is about keeping the air in the mix.

*(The music gives a pace and feel that affects the action –
makes the UTENSILS dance, makes MUM sing.)*

We want a beautiful, light cake.

A lovely melt in the mouth texture with each and every
tiny sweet crumb defined and held.

(To the implements.) That's really good.

*(Their cake-making becomes more like dancing. TEA SPOON
returns during this section.)*

When you're having one of those days where the world's
licked you clean and wants some more. Come into the
kitchen. Switch the oven on. Get the butter out of the
fridge.

(Sings.)

When you're separated
Feeling beat
Skip the main course
Keep it sweet.
Coat yourself in what is true
It's your turn to lick life's spoon.

(Sings.)

There's a cake
And you can make it –
If you want to
You can bake it.
All it takes is sugar, flour,
A bowl, a spoon – and half an hour.

(Speaks.)

Once your flour's incorporated, scrape the bowl down
again – and give it a good beating for about half a
minute.

(Sings.)

One big one
Or lots of little

It'll give you a rise,
It's a raffle prize
When you're mouth is full of cake
There's no room for anger and hate.
(*Sings.*)
There's a cake
And you can make it –
If you want to
You can bake it
All it takes is sugar, flour,
A bowl, a spoon – and half an hour.
(*Speaks.*)
This ensures that everything's mixed right through. I
don't want to bite into my cake and find there are lumps
of unmixed ingredients.
So much more than a biscuit and thicker than a crisp.
Yellow sponge with a blob of icing on – doesn't have to
be anything fancy.
(*Sings.*)
There's a cake
And you can make it –
If you want to
You can bake it
All it takes is sugar, flour,
A bowl, a spoon – and half an hour.
(*The cake is ready to go into the tins. The music continues a
little. As MUM speaks, the UTENSILS get more and more
lively and crowd round her – she is the best MUM in the
world and they love her.*)
And you should have a lovely smooth mixture, with a
nice dropping consistency.
(*They are all trying to kiss her and climb on her.*)
Spoon the cake mix into your tins.
(*The music dies away. She organises them into a line to scoop
the mixture out of the bowl and put it in the trays.*)
Make sure it's level.
(*As they help, she occasionally picks one of them up to level
the mixture, or scrape a bit more off into the tins. She doesn't
notice that they're getting tired.*)

This wants to bake for twenty minutes at gas mark 4 or 180 degrees.

(*SPATULA – carrying a massive amount of mixture – buckles under the weight. The mixture pulls him to the floor. He's stuck there, like a fly in treacle.*)

If your oven is not the right temperature, you will not get a successful bake. Baking powder reacts with heat, becoming a gas, and that's what creates your volume. If there isn't enough heat, it won't rise enough, you'll get a shallow cake, which may not even be cooked properly in the middle.

(*The others all look at MUM, but she doesn't notice. So they start scraping the mixture off him and carrying it to MUM.*)

If you heat your oven too high, the crust of the cake will crack and you'll get this volcano effect, where the crust of the cake is cooked, and the uncooked mixture inside rushes to the top and erupts out through the crust, giving you a crowning effect.

(*WOODEN SPOON and TABLE SPOON have a clash over who's carrying a bit of mixture. They fight. Still MUM doesn't notice. TEA SPOON takes the bit of mixture they're fighting over to MUM.*)

There are lots of ways to tell if your cake is ready. You can take it out and tap the bottom of the tin. If you get a dull, hollow sound, then it's ready. You can use a sharp knife and insert it into the centre of the cake. If it comes out clean, the cake is ready. If there's any uncooked mixture on your knife, give it another ten or fifteen minutes.

(*TEA SPOON is almost dead on his non-stirring end. MUM picks it up and puts its mixture in the tin. She places it back on the table – but it wants to be held. It keeps trying to jump up to her. In the end it manages, and tries to breastfeed.*)

You can press the top of the cake and if it springs back, that's a good sign it's ready.

(*MUM puts TEA SPOON down again. Again it tries – this time joined by TABLE SPOON, who has also had enough.*)

If you're making a family cake, top and fill it with butter cream – 250g of butter to 500g of icing sugar – so that's half butter to icing sugar with a few drops of vanilla essence. And give it a nice smooth coat.

(*Now when the remaining UTENSILS arrive with mixture, they lovingly spoon it onto her instead of into the tins.*)

Again, butter at room temperature. Mix until it's creamy.

(*MUM keeps trying to put all the various UTENSILS down – but they are quicker than her and soon climb up again. She can't do anything. Her movements are like someone underwater as she tries to disengage herself from them as well as do what she needs to.*)

If it's for a special occasion you can use regal icing.

(*SPATULA finally pulls itself up from the table – it wants a piece of MUM too. As it nears, MUM picks it up and uses it to level the mix. It uses all its brute force to slap itself onto MUM's cheek – and then starts to work its way down for a feed. MUM desperately wants to get to the finish now.*)

You can top it with sweets, coconut, sugar flowers, vermicelli, chocolate pieces, grated chocolate, fruit. You can pipe butter cream.

(*She tries to put them down – but as quick as she lies one down the previous one is climbing up again.*)

Fruit and chocolate go well together.

(*They won't be washed up. Won't let her put the cake in the oven. The UTENSILS will only breastfeed. Now she is trying to reach again and again for the cake – sometimes picking it up, only to have to put it down to free herself. This builds – like that game where you make a pile of hands and bring the bottom one to the top, faster and faster.*)

Don't leave it to sit.

(*At the peak of this episode, she makes a final lunge for the cake tins. She grabs one, but the other skids off down the worktop –*)

If you leave it to sit, it'll form a skin on its surface which will prevent the cake rising. This can then crack, creating the volcano effect I mentioned earlier.

(*And into the sink. She stands – covered in cake mixture and breastfeeding UTENSILS, holding the other cake tin.*)

If at that point, the cake comes into contact with warm, soapy water, the temptation is to very quickly pick it

out, drain off the worst of the water and then mix in the
remainder.
(*She does this as she speaks.*)
There are two problems with this approach. One: the
action of the soap on the other ingredients. And two: the
action of the water on the ingredients.
(*She moves to the bin.*)
At this point in the recipe it's important to realise that –
no matter how long you mix it for or how long and at
what temperature you cook it, or how level it is in the
tin – this is no longer a cake.
(*She drops one cake tin into the bin.*)
It no longer has cake potential.
(*She drops the other cake tin into the bin.*)
It should now be dealt with as an item of housewifery –
housewifery being across the tracks from baking,
concerning itself not with edible matter in relation to
receptacles and utensils but receptacles and utensils in
relation to edible matter.
And the removal thereof.
Which should always be complete.
(*The UTENSILS start to fall asleep – fall from her body
with great grace, like Autumn leaves. There is music. She
catches each one, washes it, and settles them to sleep in a tea-
towel bed.*)

Scene 2

MUM: Swiss Roll.
(*MUM goes to a cupboard and opens it. She gets out a swiss
roll tin. She doesn't close the cupboard properly.*
*MUM talks very quietly. She doesn't want to wake the
UTENSILS. She works very quickly – she knows she doesn't
have much time. She cleans and orders as she goes.*)
This is very quick. It has to be made very quickly. Once
you've started it, you can't leave it – you have to keep
going.
(*She puts a pan of water onto the ring.*)

I'm heating a pan of water on the stove, into which I'm putting another pan, to create a Bain-Marie.
(*She puts a bowl on top.*
JOHN, a big doll with lots of hair and a dress, peeps out of the cupboard. It looks at MUM, then at the audience.)
You can fill the swiss roll with jam, jam and cream, buttercream or crème patissierre – which is like a baked custard.
(*JOHN goes back into the cupboard again.*)
I'm going to mix 50g of plain flour with a half a teaspoon of baking powder.
(*She does so.*
JOHN peeps out of the cupboard again.)
You'll find that professional bakers always make cakes with their hands.
(*This time JOHN comes out of the cupboard. He comes over to MUM. He watches for a while as MUM opens her fingers and shows us.*)
Whisk.
(*She closes her fingers and shows us.*)
Spoon.

JOHN: What are you doing, Mummy?

MUM: Making cake.

JOHN: What are you doing?

MUM: Putting the sugar on the scales, John.

JOHN: What's sugar, Mummy?

MUM: It's a sweetener. And a colourant. It gives the cake that golden colour. It's very important. Without it the cake won't get made. (*To us.*) You can use granulated sugar for most cakes, but for any mixture that needs creaming a finer sugar will work better. I'm using caster sugar.

JOHN: Are you like sugar?

MUM: Can you just speak a bit more quietly.

JOHN: Why?

MUM: The spoons are asleep. No, I'm not like sugar. (*To us.*) Sugar is a liquid which comes from sugar beet or sugar cane which is dried in a sugar refinery into crystals.

JOHN: Without you the cake won't get made.

MUM: (*To us.*) Then into the Bain-Marie I'm going to put three eggs and the 50g of caster sugar.

JOHN: Can I help, Mummy?

MUM: No, John. I've got to get it made quickly.

JOHN: What are scales?

MUM: They're for finding out how heavy things are.

JOHN: How heavy am I?

MUM: You're about one kilo.

(*JOHN stands on the scales.*)

JOHN: How heavy am I?

MUM: Two point five kilos. (*To us.*) For the Swiss Roll you'll need a seven by eleven-inch oblong swiss roll tin.

JOHN: I could help.

MUM: It's just that you tend to slow things down.

JOHN: Why, Mummy?

MUM: Because you're not very good at it. You can grease this tin. Put a bit of butter in it.

(*MUM sets JOHN up greasing the tin as she speaks to the audience.*)

(*To us.*) The tin needs to be greased and have a piece of greaseproof paper lining the bottom.

JOHN: I'm not very good at this.

MUM: (*To us.*) The greaseproof should have tails on it, so it's easy to use to pull the Swiss Roll out with.

JOHN: My arms only do that.

(*JOHN does an up and down motion with his arms.*)

MUM: I know, John.

JOHN: Can I do something else?

MUM: (*To us.*) What I then do is lay a clean tea towel on the table, with a piece of greaseproof paper on top.

JOHN: Something that utilizes this movement?

(*Does up and down movement as MUM continues – still stirring the Bain-Marie.*)

MUM: (*To us.*) Sprinkle sugar on it and then tip the finished cake out onto the sugar. (*To JOHN.*) I don't know if there's anything we need that movement for.

JOHN: You're telling me this movement – (*He does the movement again.*) – is completely redundant in cake-making?

MUM: (*To us.*) The heat will absorb the sugar, you can then take the tin off, pull the greaseproof paper off.

JOHN: Or this.

(*He turns his arm right round in a circle.*)

MUM: (*To us.*) Then roll it up using the tea towel and greaseproof paper underneath. (*To JOHN.*) Don't do that.

JOHN: Could that movement be useful to you in any way?

(*He turns his arm right round again.*)

MUM: (*To us.*) The greaseproof paper helps to keep in the moisture and keep it pliable. (*To JOHN.*) Please don't do that.

(*He spins his arm round and round.*)

JOHN: I really want to help.

MUM: I know you do.

JOHN: Do you like cake?

MUM: I love cake. (*To us.*) You can see now that the sugar is beginning to melt.

JOHN: You love cake.

(*She shows the audience the pan.*)

Why are you making a cake?

MUM: Because cake is a good thing and everybody loves cake. It's lovely for us all to have a cake.

(*He starts to try and organise the greaseproof paper.*)

JOHN: I love you. Do you love me?

MUM: I love you, John.

JOHN: You said you love cake.

MUM: That's different.

JOHN: So there are two forms of love.

(*MUM continues over JOHN.*)

A love of inanimate objects, and a love of animate, thinking objects – like me.

MUM: (*To us.*) For a deep cake, you would grease and line the bottom and the sides.

JOHN: I am unable to do this task for you.

MUM: (*To us.*) For this, you only need line the base, and flour and grease the sides of your tin.

JOHN: I would *love* to do it, but I am unable to.

(*JOHN is completely covered with a huge roll of greaseproof, he rattles and shakes, trying to get out.)*

Mummy! I can't get out!

MUM: (*To us.*) I'm beating the eggs into the sugar now.

JOHN: Help me, mummy! Everything's gone greaseproof!
(*MUM takes the greaseproof off him as she passes and quickly cuts out the right shape and puts it on the tin.*)
I thought I'd never get out of there.

MUM: You're out now.

JOHN: I thought I'd had it.

MUM: (*To us.*) And as the eggs and sugar mix, the eggs are cooking at the same time.

JOHN: What is love?

MUM: It's a big cuddle.

JOHN: So I take it you'll be cuddling me very soon.

MUM: When I've finished the cake.

JOHN: By this you imply you love cake more than me.

MUM: I just want to get something finished. I have to get something finished.

JOHN: You don't have to.

MUM: I just want to get this one thing done.

JOHN: Want is the key word. You want.

MUM: (*To us.*) You may have noticed that I haven't added any butter to this recipe.

JOHN: How does this love I have for helping you and the love you have for the cake compare with – for example – your love for me?

MUM: My love for you is deeper.

JOHN: Like a deeper cake – there's more of it.

MUM: (*Whispers.*) More of it, yes. And that's because this is a fatless sponge.

JOHN: More of it than the more shallow love you have for the fatless sponge.

MUM: (*Whispers.*) Less shallow, yes.

JOHN: (*Whispers.*) Why are you whispering?

MUM: (*Whispers.*) Because the spoons are asleep.

JOHN: (*Whispers.*) I love you.

MUM: (*Whispers to us.*) It needs eating the same day it's made.

JOHN: You love me.

MUM: If you want it to last longer, you can add some fat.

JOHN: And yet not one of us is happy.

MUM: The spoons are happy.

JOHN: The spoons are asleep.

(JOHN goes over to where the spoons are sleeping.)

And I think the question of whether happiness and sleep are the same thing falls outside the remit of this conversation.

(JOHN starts to stamp and jump near to the spoons.)

MUM: You'll wake the spoons up.

(JOHN and MUM both speak to the audience.)

JOHN: *(To us.)* Why am I trying to wake the spoons up?

MUM: *(To us.)* What I'm looking for is that when I trail the mixture into itself, I can see the trail it leaves like ribbons –

JOHN: I don't want the spoons awake.

MUM: And the trails should stay for a little while.

JOHN: I want to be the only thing in the world.

MUM: That way you know the batter's ready.

JOHN: But I am not the only thing in the world. There are spoons.

(He turns to them.)

And there is cake.

(He turns to it.)

MUM: While you're waiting for the eggs and sugar to get to that ribbon stage, it's a good idea to think ahead over the next few days or weeks.

JOHN: I am treading a thin line between two kinds of agony.

MUM: And plan menus: Monday – sausage and mash, Tuesday: pasta in a tomato sauce with peas.

JOHN: Cake or spoons.

MUM: Wednesday: Mexican – question mark?

JOHN: Spoons or cake?

MUM: Or if you feel that's beyond you, make a mental list of those people who've phoned you over the last three weeks whose calls you have not returned.

JOHN: And where am I in this? What about me?

(*JOHN stamps his feet – he still speaks to us.*)

MUM: That's about ready.

JOHN: I don't want to feel like this, you see. I'd rather wake the spoons up than feel like this. I'd rather ruin everything than feel like this.

MUM: John?

JOHN: Yes, Mummy?

MUM: Would you go and get the sieve from the end of the table for me? (*To us.*) You're going to take the pan from the heat.

(*JOHN gets it and brings it back.*)

JOHN: I love you, Mummy.

MUM: I love you, John. (*To us.*) Once you've done that –

JOHN: Do you love me more than eggs?

MUM: Yes, I love you more than eggs. (*To us.*) Recall the birthdays and ages of all your family members and which of those you've marked with a card or present in the last two-years.

JOHN: Do you love me more than the oven?

MUM: Yes I love you more than the oven. (*To us.*) And berate yourself.

JOHN: Do you love me more than cake?

MUM: Yes I love you more than cake.

JOHN: I love you more than cake. I love you more than the spoons.

MUM: I love you as much as the spoons.

JOHN: But not more than the spoons?

MUM: So before I preheat the oven, I'm going to pause.

(*JOHN deliberately trips on the spoons.*)

Think: 'What am I doing?'

JOHN: I've really hurt my foot.

MUM: 'Why am I doing this?'

JOHN: I've really hurt my foot. The spoons tripped me up.

(*MUM kisses his foot.*)

MUM: 'Who am I doing this for?'

JOHN: I love you.

MUM: I love you too.

JOHN: I think I need a cuddle.

MUM: (*To us.*) A Swiss Roll needs a very hot oven and it

only needs to bake for twelve minutes.

JOHN: How do you know you love me?

MUM: Because I feel it.

JOHN: How do you feel?

MUM: I feel warm.

JOHN: How can I know you feel warm?

MUM: Because I show you.

JOHN: Because a lot of the time you seem either very angry with me or very tired of me. You seem to want me to stop what I'm doing and either go away or to go to sleep and you want, in fact, to engage in some activity that cannot and does not have me at its centre.

MUM: I would do anything for you.

JOHN: Anything?

MUM: I would die for you, John.

JOHN: You would die for me but would you give me a cuddle?

(*JOHN looks at the audience. He picks up an egg.*)

MUM: So I'm going to preheat the oven to 180 degrees or Gas Mark 4.

(*He walks to the edge of the table. During the following exchange he wanders close to the edge of the table – and holds the egg over. MUM isn't watching, she's entirely absorbed with the cake and her public performance.*)

It needs to bake quickly as there's no stability in the mix – when you see it's golden brown, it's done.

(*He drops the egg. It smashes on the floor. JOHN looks at it. Now he starts to peer over the edge with intent.*)

Now you're ready to sieve the flour.

(*JOHN steps off the table into mid-air. He does a cartoon legs wiggling in mid-air thing – looks back at the table, looks at the audience.*)

JOHN: Mummy!

MUM: What are you doing?

(*Then falls, legs arms and head all twisted round – on the audience side of the counter.*)

JOHN: I can't get up.

MUM: Give me your hand.

JOHN: I could give you a leg.

MUM: (*To us.*) Don't forget to smile. Smiling always makes
a better cake.
(*MUM hauls him up.*)
What are you doing?
JOHN: I suppose I'm testing the depth of your love.
MUM: Why don't you help me make the cake?
JOHN: Are you exploiting me?
MUM: You like pouring things.
JOHN: Am I exploited by making the cake?
MUM: We're doing it together.
JOHN: Does this prove the profundity of your love for me?
Or am I being prostituted to your love of cake?
MUM: Don't say prostituted, John.
(*JOHN looks at the audience.*)
Do you want to help?
JOHN: I really want to help in any way I can.
MUM: Now I'm going to sieve the flour and baking powder
mixture into the batter.
JOHN: I *love* to be useful. (*To us.*) That's a different form of
love.
MUM: This is fun. (*To us.*) And fold in the flour as you
sieve it in.
JOHN: It's fun.
MUM: It's a lot of fun. No lumps in the mixture.
JOHN: It's fun.
(*JOHN is sieving flour.*)
MUM: Gently fold it in.
(*MUM folds it in with a beater.*
JOHN blows into the flour – making a big cloud.)
JOHN: I'm having fun, you see.
MUM: You might like to use a metal spoon for this.
JOHN: This is fun.
(*He blows the flour.*)
I'm making cake!
I'm having fun.
I am in the act of having fun.
(*He blows the flour twice.*)
I can make cake too!

We are making the cake
We seem to have found happiness.
We are in the act of *loving* making the cake.
(*He blows the flour again.*)
Are you happy, mummy?
MUM: Yes, I am.
(*He blows the flour.*)
JOHN: Yes.
(*He blows the flour.*)
Yes.
(*He blows the flour.*)
Yes.
(*MUM grabs the sieve from him, shouting.*)
MUM: Can you not do that anymore!
(*A moment.*)
JOHN: Did the happiness stop, Mummy? Did it stop?
MUM: Yes it did.
JOHN: At what point did the happiness stop?
(*MUM tries to regain control of the cake.*)
Because there was a lot of happiness for a long time and
now suddenly there is no happiness.
MUM: I'm just going to finish folding this flour in.
JOHN: Is it over? Has it gone? Has the happiness gone,
Mummy? The sieving gone?
MUM: We're doing mixing now.
JOHN: I'm not doing mixing.
MUM: No, you're watching.
JOHN: I would rather participate. Participation I found
brought me more happiness.
MUM: This is supposed to be a quick cake.
JOHN: If I hold the beater –
(*He does.*)
MUM: I have to get this in the oven.
JOHN: And you turn the bowl.
(*She does.*)
MUM: (*To us.*) This isn't the most efficient way of doing it –
JOHN: No, but it might return us to a state of happiness.
Turn the bowl.
That's it!

That's it!

(*MUM stops turning the bowl.*)

MUM: And put the mixture into the tin.

(*She puts the mixture in the tin.*)

JOHN: Where has the happiness gone, Mummy?

MUM: We've just put it to one side for a moment to enable us to finish the cake.

JOHN: Is that wise?

MUM: When your Swiss Roll is baked, it'll be pale golden brown and shrinking away from the edges of the tin.

JOHN: (*To us.*) What happened then? (*To MUM.*) Do you still love me, Mummy?

MUM: I always love you. (*To us.*) Once it's baked you must roll it straight away.

JOHN: Do you love me as much as you did when we were happy?

MUM: (*To us.*) If you go off to answer the phone, it'll be hard as a biscuit by the time you come back and instead of rolling, it'll break.

JOHN: When the cake is in the tin, do you love it as much as when it's in the bowl? Is it better? Do you love me more if I am in the bowl? (*He stands in the bowl.*) Or on the table. (*He stands on the table.*) If I am on the eggs. (*He stands on the eggs in the egg box.*) If I jump on the eggs. Do you love me then? (*He jumps on the eggs.*) Do you love me more if I jump on the eggs?

MUM: No!

(*She grabs him off the eggs.*)

(*To us.*) Tilt it to get it completely even. And then into the oven –

JOHN: Or do you love the cake more in the oven?

MUM: And then into your preheated oven –

JOHN: Do you love me more if I'm in the oven?

MUM: But before you do that, you might want to climb onto your worksurface –

(*She does this, as she says it.*)

JOHN: You put cake on my dress.

MUM: And then bend your legs –

(*She bends her legs.*)

JOHN: Do you love the cake on my dress more than you love the cake in the bowl?

MUM: Unless you've got enough room on your worktop to straighten them out.

JOHN: Do you love the cake on my dress more than you love my dress?

MUM: I love your dress.

JOHN: Do you love my dress more than you love me?

MUM: Get your body flat on the worktop and just let your head rest on your arm –

(*MUM is asleep.*)

JOHN: Mummy?

Mummy?

I love you.

I love you. I love love love you.

(*Still asleep, MUM hooks her arm around JOHN, pulling him across her body. She's holding him by his neck. He can't escape. His legs kick in the air.*)

Mummy.

Let go.

Let go.

I do love you.

I do.

Let go.

(*Legs in the air, waving.*)

I love you, Mummy.

I love you more than cake.

I love you more than my dress.

(*JOHN is still.*)

Scene 3

TEA SPOON wakes up. It stands up. It goes over to MUM and taps her knee. It goes to her face – trailing through the tin of cake mix. It gets some cake mix and offers it to MUM. MUM stirs. Confident she isn't dead, it goes back to the others and wakes them.

Music begins, like a film underscore. TABLE SPOON and TEA SPOON begin to climb her, like a mountain. It's an expedition.

From the other side of the counter, WOODEN SPOON and SPATULA appear, making the ascent from the opposite side.

They climb up MUM. When they get to the top, they are shocked and distressed to find they are not the only team making the ascent.

There is a face-off – metal versus wooden. It becomes like Fight Club, one on one fighting. WOODEN SPOON headbutts TABLE SPOON. TABLE SPOON falls to the ground. TEA SPOON comes over and wallops WOODEN SPOON.

The WOODEN army retreat. They find some flour and hurl a spoonful. The METAL army retreat and do the same – persuading LADLE to join them. As the flour flies, MUM becomes covered – a white mountain. And it's this landscape they're battling for, hiding behind, jumping out from. MUM stays asleep.

And the cake – still held in MUM's outstretched hand – gets destroyed: whisked, flour falls into it. It's a complete mess.

The METAL army roll a rolling pin over MUM to flatten the Metal Army. TEA SPOON gets the whisk and advances with it, like a canon. The WOODEN army retreat, only to return flying in the sieve, raining down sugar. Again the METAL army retreat. This time TEA SPOON gets an egg and flies over MUM using the whisk as a helicopter. The WOODEN army flee. The egg falls into MUM's Swiss Roll mixture and she wakes up. She stands up on the work surface, the cake tin still in one hand. She is covered in cake mixture, but doesn't seem to notice.

MUM: Because you've greased your tin, this will stop the sides and bottom of the cake becoming over-brown, and will also make it easier to remove from the tin.
(*She continues, as if this is part of the same thought.*)
Who did this?
(*The UTENSILS look at her. She looks at the cake in her hand.*)
Who did this?
(*She turns to the LADLE.*)
Was it you?
(*TEA SPOON steps forward a little.*)

Well you can clean it up.
(*They all look at her.*)
Go on.
Or I'll put you in your drawer and you won't come out
at lunchtime and you won't come out at tea-time – no
yogurt, no soup, no sugar in tea – you'll stay in there all
night and you won't come out until breakfast time
tomorrow and then we'll have toast.
(*Their tidying is not very good. They start to spoon the
ingredients back into the bags. But as they cannot also hold
the bags, this happens very slowly and with little accuracy.*)
(*To us.*) It's always useful to remind yourself: What cake
am I making? (*To them.*) You're putting the sugar into the
flour bag. (*To us.*) What recipe am I following? (*To them.*)
What's this? This is flour? And sugar. (*To us.*) Mixing
your ingredients like this, before they're weighed is
never a good idea.
(*MUM brushes flour from her shoulder – seemingly ignoring
the fact she's completely covered and just paying attention to
this one area. She brushes her hair and a cloud of flour rises
from it.*)
(*To them.*) It's going all over the floor.
(*Their flour scraping becomes more manic.*)
It's going all over the floor.
In the bag.
Stop!
(*She pushes the big mixing bowl towards WOODEN SPOON.*)
Take it away.
(*WOODEN SPOON looks at her.*)
Go on.
(*WOODEN SPOON inches the bowl down to the sink. It is
very hard work. It reaches the edge of the sink.*)
In the sink.
(*WOODEN SPOON and the bowl both plunge into the sink.
SPATULA starts the scraping again. As MUM continues, we
see the bowl capsize – to WOODEN SPOON's horror.*)
(*To us.*) And even if this is a recipe you have followed
many times before –

(*She picks SPATULA up and slams it down on the table.*)

It's always the first time you've made this cake.

(*As MUM continues, UTENSILS start to notice what's happening and alert each other.*)

Every cake is different.

(*WOODEN SPOON is drowning. The UTENSILS try to alert MUM. One of them throws WOODEN SPOON a washing up sponge as a life buoy – but that sinks.*)

And as you keep adding your ingredients you may have the feeling that – no matter how familiar you are with your quantities and methods –

(*We see WOODEN SPOON trying to climb out of the sink, but slipping down again. The other UTENSILS are going backwards and forwards to MUM. MUM picks one of them up.*)

In all this addition, addition, addition there will somewhere be a subtraction.

(*She goes to the sink with it.*)

Something you haven't accounted for

(*MUM sees WOODEN SPOON sinking under the water. A still moment. MUM puts the other implement down.*)

No!

(*MUM leans into the sink, trying to reach WOODEN SPOON who is in the depths.*)

Get my hand. Get hold of my hand!

(*She leans further and further in – *)

No!

(*She plunges her head into the water. Silence. MUM is under the water. The other UTENSILS watch and wait around the sink. They are shocked as she bursts up for air and then plunges back down again. Again they watch, comforting each other. SPATULA alone, taking it hard.*

Their hopes for WOODEN SPOON are beginning to fade.

Then MUM comes up – holding WOODEN SPOON close to her.

She blows on WOODEN SPOON, rubbing it, trying to revive it. WOODEN SPOON starts to move slightly. It's alive.

SPATULA – in a rare show of emotion – pushes a tea towel

across the table to her. She dries WOODEN SPOON and herself. SPATULA starts to scrape the flour that coats the work-surface into piles – efficiently. The other UTENSILS scoop it up and move it into one big pile. Meanwhile, MUM rocks, holding WOODEN SPOON.

UTENSILS are skating now. A couple – one metal, one wooden. SPATULA – scraping end down like a skirt – skates alone. They skate beautifully – sometimes together, sometimes as a loving couple and one alone. They jump and twirl. MUM watches them. They come over. MUM looks at WOODEN SPOON and gently places it down to dance with SPATULA. As the dance continues – once we have understood and journeyed with its beauty – JOHN climbs up from behind the counter where he has been left, ignored.)

JOHN: You're wondering why I haven't said anything for a while.

I'm having a bit of time out.

I'm having a bit of a think.

I've got a lot of thinking to do.

(*The dance ends.*)

I'm having a good think.

MUM: Pineapple Upside Down Cake.

(*MUM starts to get the ingredients together.*)

We're not looking for a very light sponge here, something more dense is fine –

JOHN: I'm beginning to think that things are slotting into place for me.

MUM: It's essentially a pudding, more of a pudding than a cake.

JOHN: There's Mummy.

MUM: So I'm just going to chuck all the ingredients in together.

JOHN: The Spoons and their friends.

(*The UTENSILS buzz around in a group.*)

MUM: Butter, sugar –

JOHN: Cake.

MUM: Eggs, flour.

JOHN: Love.

(*She goes and looks in the fridge.*)

MUM: Then a pineapple – half a pineapple cut into rings.
(*She pours the contents of an already opened tin onto the work surface.*)

JOHN: Happiness. And me. John.

MUM: And about eight glace cherries.
(*She gets them. As she gets them from the back shelf, JOHN kicks the pineapple chunks to the floor. All the UTENSILS rush over to look.*)

JOHN: That wasn't exactly premeditated, but I did have a good think about it.
(*MUM returns.*)

MUM: I'm going to wash the cherries to get all the glucose syrup off them.
(*She does this. The UTENSILS are very worried about the pineapple. MUM sees it on the floor. MUM looks round at the UTENSILS who all skid away across the worktop, fearful of what she might do.*)
And then I'm going to line them up on the worktop. The straighter the line the better. And then, with my fist, with the base of my hand, crush them.
(*She crushes one – the UTENSILS jump.*)
One at a time. And if we say that the first one's wanting.
(*She crushes another – the UTENSILS jump again.*)
And that this one's not wanting.
(*She crushes another – the UTENSILS jump.*
As she continues, the UTENSILS huddle together.)
This one's bleakness.
This one's weeping.
This one's looking ahead.
This one's looking backwards.
This one's sudden catastrophe.
This one's carefulness.
(*MUM looks as though she might completely break down. She seems unable to go on. The UTENSILS huddle together again – and then they get the packet of butter and bring it over to MUM. They look at her hopefully. WOODEN SPOON hops into her hand. It wriggles hopefully. MUM pulls herself together.*)

This is Everything-you've-ever-wanted-in-life-smothered-in-cream-and-chocolate Cake. Starting with the same principle as the sponge, we're going to cream the butter and the sugar – 150g of butter and 100g of sugar. But we're going to do something different when it comes to the egg.

(*JOHN looks at the audience.*

The UTENSILS measure the butter and sugar, and cream them together.

The UTENSILS make the cake efficiently, helping MUM at every turn.)

JOHN: What's egg?

MUM: It's something a hen lays.

(*A couple of UTENSILS stop to look at JOHN as they pass. He kicks one so it spins in the air before landing further down the worktop. MUM doesn't notice. The other one rushes over to it and watches as it picks itself up and they go over to melt the chocolate in a Bain-Marie that they've set up.*)

Sometimes they hatch and a chicken comes out and sometimes they don't and we use them in cakes.

(*To us.*) Then melt 100g of chocolate. I always use couverture chocolate, which is the absolute crème de la crème of chocolate. It'll give you a much better colour than cocoa, and a much, much better real chocolate taste.

(*The UTENSILS start bringing a box of eggs over.*

JOHN takes one from the box. They continue to MUM.)

JOHN: How do you know there isn't a chicken in there?

MUM: Because there wasn't a hen sitting on it. And it's not been fertilized.

(*JOHN looks at the audience.*

The UTENSILS return for the final egg.)

(*To us.*) To the buttercream I'm going to add the yolks of six eggs. Just the yolks. The whites we're going to separate out.

(*MUM separates the eggs as the UTENSILS get the final egg from JOHN.*)

JOHN: Who fertilized the egg?

MUM: No-one fertilized this egg.

JOHN: The one with the chicken in.

MUM: The daddy chicken. The cockerel.

(*He lets them get it onto TABLE SPOON, then picks up WOODEN SPOON and smashes the egg, then puts the spoon down again.*)

There should be no white in the yolks, but more importantly no yolk in the whites – or they won't whip into peaks.

JOHN: Can the daddy chicken fertilise you?

MUM: No.

(*The UTENSILS scoop what they can of the egg onto TABLE SPOON and take it to MUM.*)

JOHN: Do you lay eggs?

MUM: No. I'm a person, I don't lay eggs.

JOHN: Can you be fertilised?

MUM: Yes, yes I can.

JOHN: Could you make a cake if you were?

MUM: No – I don't make cakes with my eggs. I'm not a hen.

(*The UTENSILS arrive with their smashed egg.*)

What happened here?

(*The UTENSILS don't answer. MUM clears it up.*)

That's wasted now, that egg.

(*The UTENSILS look shifty.*)

If you're not more careful I won't let you do eggs.

(*The UTENSILS go on their way.*)

JOHN: Do you like being a Mummy?

MUM: Yes.

JOHN: Do you like making cakes?

MUM: Yes.

JOHN: You don't seem very happy.

MUM: (*To us.*) You need to preheat the oven to gas mark 4 or 180 degrees.

(*The UTENSILS go to do it, but MUM stops them.*)

I'll do it.

(*MUM goes to the oven, JOHN goes over to her. The UTENSILS continue with the cake.*)

JOHN: Could a chicken do that?

MUM: No.

JOHN: Why do you put it in the oven?

MUM: Because it'll rise – that's what makes it into a cake.
At the moment it's just mixture.

JOHN: If you put an egg in the oven, will it rise?

MUM: No.

JOHN: If you put a chicken in the oven will it rise?

MUM: No, it'll cook.

JOHN: If you put me in the oven, will I rise?

MUM: No, John, you'd melt.

> (*JOHN looks at the audience.*)
> (*To us.*) Now I'm beating the egg whites.
> (*MUM whisks the egg whites.*)
> We're going to beat them to a half-way stage – so they're not very stiff. And then add 75g of sugar.
> (*As MUM continues, JOHN starts to threaten the UTENSILS again – trying to herd them towards the oven. Music underscores their action.*
> *The UTENSILS join together to become a BIRD to cope with JOHN. It pecks at him – now they're more equally matched.*)

MUM: (*To us.*) You might have one hand free, or you might have no hands free. You might find that although you want to make a perfect cake for your children, you cannot even remember the name for the thing that you get eggs out of.

JOHN: A hen, Mummy.

MUM: (*To us.*) The hen where you get eggs and butter and milk and sometimes pickle and salad. That hen that keeps things cold with the little light that comes on when you open it.

> (*As MUM continues, the BIRD flies onto MUM's shoulder. MUM pets it, without really registering it.*)
> It's important to add the sugar at this stage, otherwise it'll just settle at the bottom of the bowl. And continue to beat until the egg whites are peaking. And you might ask yourself, when you cannot remember the name for a hen, how you will ever be able to make a light, even, streakless, faultless cake for your children.

JOHN: Mummy? Why am I like this?

MUM: It's the way you're made, John.

> (*JOHN lunges for the BIRD, a spoon falls from it. JOHN uses the spoon to stab at the BIRD – the BIRD pecks back, flying and landing around the room to escape him.*)

JOHN: Is it because I'm a hen?

MUM: No, John, you're not a hen. If you find you are having doubts about the cake, you might want to put them to one side while you –

JOHN: Do I have life?

MUM: Yes.

> (*The BIRD changes back into spoons now JOHN's focus has shifted. The egg whites are now whipped to peaks.*)

(*To us.*) While you mix the melted chocolate and the buttercream.

> (*The UTENSILS have brought the chocolate mixture. They do as she says – mixing the chocolate and the buttercream. JOHN turns both his arms round a few times. Then his head.*)

You might find you have to put your own children to one side while you –

JOHN: Can you do this, Mummy?

MUM: No, I don't think I can. While you very slowly and lightly incorporate the meringue into the batter.

> (*JOHN continues to turn his head round.*)

JOHN: Why not?

MUM: Stop than, John.

> (*JOHN stops with his head the wrong way round.*)

(*To the UTENSILS.*) Very slowly.

(*To JOHN.*) Your head's the wrong way round.

JOHN: I don't care.

> (*JOHN continues to turn his head round.*
> *As MUM continues, we see the UTENSILS, some with chocolate hairstyles and some with whisked egg white hairstyles as they stand around, taking turns to scoop and mix.*)

(*To us.*) You can leave the two parts of the mixture separate for about ten to fifteen minutes, but once you start to mix them together, you have to be quick.

> (*JOHN whizzes his head round a few more times, stopping with it backwards again.*)

MUM: (*To us.*) You might want to remind yourself that –
(*She grabs JOHN's head and wrestles with him to turn it the right way round.*)

JOHN: Get off –

MUM: (*To us.*) Cake-making is an exciting and fulfilling art –

JOHN: Get off my head!

MUM: (*To us.*) And something you can quickly excel at.
(*MUM succeeds in getting JOHN's head the right way round.*)

JOHN: Are there other Mummys, Mummy?

MUM: Yes there are.

JOHN: Like you?

MUM: Perhaps not quite like me. (*To us.*) Try not to give in to feelings that somehow you don't have all the ingredients you need. Weigh out 150g of flour next.

JOHN: What is flour?

MUM: It's ground wheat. It's part of the wheat grain, ground up. (*To us.*) Or that if you do have all the ingredients, you are perhaps not following the right recipe. Add one teaspoon of baking powder.

JOHN: Are there other children?

MUM: Yes there are, John. (*To us.*) And fold it in. Flour is made from the purest part of the wheat grain. The endosperm.

JOHN: Like me?

MUM: (*To JOHN.*) Perhaps not quite like you, John. It contains gluten which, when it gets wet, goes like chewing gum and binds the mix together.

JOHN: Do you make cake for them, Mummy?

MUM: I make cake for you, John.

JOHN: What about all the other children? Do you make cake for them?

MUM: No.

JOHN: Why not?

MUM: Because I haven't got enough eggs. Flour is like a building block. One of cake-makings basics.

JOHN: Am I a basic, Mummy?

MUM: No, you're a luxury. (*To us.*) I'm using grammes because by rights pounds and ounces are no longer in existence.

JOHN: Is existence a luxury, Mummy?

MUM: No, existence is a basic.

JOHN: Do I exist, Mummy?

MUM: Yes. Why don't you hold this sieve?
(*JOHN takes the sieve and holds it over his face.*)

MUM: Then into two six or seven inch prepared tins.
(*MUM puts half the mixture into a tin.*)

JOHN: I am gone. I am no more.
(*Takes it away.*)

MUM: Into one I'm putting the beautiful, happy potential of cake –

JOHN: Now I am here. (*Puts it over his face.*) Now I am gone.

MUM: You can't go off at this point and have a cup of tea – this mixture cannot rest. The aeration caused by the meringue will escape from the mix leaving you with gooey bits in your cake.
(*JOHN takes the sieve off.*)

JOHN: Now I am John.

MUM: And it won't rise properly. It'll be too dense.
(*JOHN puts the sieve back.*)

JOHN: Now I am gone.

MUM: Into this one I'm putting the nagging feeling that there is another recipe.
(*MUM puts the remaining mixture into the other tin.*)

JOHN: Now I am John.

MUM: Another recipe that I haven't tried before – another way. (*To us.*) You're losing air all the time it's not in the oven – air is escaping from the mix and it won't rise, it'll be dense and gooey and that's not what we're trying to achieve.
(*MUM puts the tins into the oven, talking as JOHN does.*)
And into your hot, preheated oven.

JOHN: I'm gone.
(*He takes the sieve away.*)
Now I am John.

MUM: This is about the time to start thinking about what goes in the middle. What will you use to stick these things together, to connect them, to make them a whole? (*MUM gets icing sugar and butter out – the UTENSILS are excited.*

JOHN puts the sieve back over his face. As the action continues, MUM prepares the filling and covering.)

JOHN: Now I am no more.

MUM: John –

JOHN: The cake exists, but do I?

MUM: (*Shouts.*) John, will you please be quiet for a minute!

JOHN: You shouted at me.

You're a bitch.

Bitch bitch bitch.

MUM: You go down the other end of the table.

JOHN: Bitch!

MUM: Go on.

(*JOHN goes.*)

(*To us.*) If you want something really chocolatey, you could enrobe it with a ganache, made from fresh cream and real chocolate pieces melted together, which will give you a wonderful shiny surface onto which you can stick whatever you choose. Or you could fill it with butter cream – and cover it as well. You can put chocolate butter cream inside. Or cream.

(*At the other end of the worktop, JOHN starts to get at the UTENSILS. MUM doesn't notice.*)

But you might feel that's not enough. You might feel that cream isn't enough to hold this thing together. When cake doesn't stop your own children hitting each other and wanting to kill each other, and you sometimes doubt your own ability to stop yourself hitting your own children. When even though you don't have enough eggs to make cake for all the children, you know that you are not a bad person and nor are your children or any of the other children and cake is such a good thing.

(*JOHN catches SPATULA. MUM doesn't notice.*)

I'm mixing 250g of butter with 500g of icing sugar to make buttercream, and replacing 50g of sugar with 50g of cocoa for chocolate buttercream.

(*MUM is mixing the icing with TABLE SPOON.*)
I'm just creaming this together, gradually adding the sugar to the mix.
(*JOHN closes in on WOODEN SPOON.*)
JOHN: (*Deep voice.*) Come on – come to Daddy.
(*He catches it. It desperately tried to escape – putting up quite a fight, but JOHN doesn't let go. The butter icing is ready. JOHN goes to the oven.*)
MUM: (*To us.*) To pipe designs onto a cake, you need icing nozzles with a bag to hold the icing.
(*She starts scooping the plain buttercream into a piping bag, using TABLE SPOON.*)
Icing nozzles are available in lots of different designs, I'm using a number 21, which will give me small star shapes.
(*JOHN puts SPATULA and WOODEN SPOON into the oven. He shuts the door.*
TEA SPOON comes over to MUM to alert her attention. MUM takes no notice. We hear a knocking from the oven – nothing much, just a knock.)
If you're not confident about using the bag, you can practice on an upturned plate first.
(*We hear another knock. As the text continues, TEA SPOON tells TABLE SPOON what's happened and they both try to tell MUM – but MUM just keeps picking them up and using them for the icing.*)
Once the icing is in the bag, I'm going to ensure all the air's out, twist the open end up to stop it escaping once I begin – and also to stop the icing drying out and hardening before I'm ready to use it.
(*There is a frantic banging from the oven as the UTENSILS try to get out.*)
If you want, you can use royal icing to pipe more complex flowers onto greaseproof paper and let them dry.
(*Now there is no sound from the oven at all.*)
But as this is a family cake, I'm just going to use buttercream.

(*Ding! The cake is ready. MUM goes to the oven. She takes the tins out and puts them on the worktop.*)

Take your cake out of the oven, cool it slightly – leave it to stand for a couple of minutes while you get on with something else –

(*She finds the UTENSILS.*)

Aaaaaaagh!

(*She is frozen for a moment.*)

What are you doing in there?

How did this happen?

(*She tries to take them out – they are blackened and very hot – really too hot to hold.*)

Aah!

(*She scalds herself getting them out – upset and angry at the same time.*)

You stupid spoons.

JOHN: Stupid spoons.

(*She grabs them out and runs to the sink. TEA SPOON and TABLE SPOON follow, worried.*)

MUM: What did you think you were doing?

(*She puts one under the tap – it writhes. TEA SPOON and TABLE SPOON find this very distressing – they turn away. The other UTENSIL writhes on the worktop.*)

How did this happen?

JOHN: It wouldn't happen if you lavished us with love and attention every minute of the day instead of making cake.

(*As she talks, she wets a teatowel and cools the UTENSILS down with it.*)

MUM: I'm loving you and making cake.

JOHN: What about what we want? You're not interested in what we want.

MUM: (*To the UTENSILS.*) Who's idea was this? (*To us.*) Cake making is a set of tasks done in a particular order.

(*TEA SPOON, aided by TABLE SPOON, starts to pipe 'JOHN' in icing on the wall behind JOHN.*)

JOHN: You're interested in what we should want.

MUM: I'm not interested in what you should want.

(*SPATULA resists the cloth.*)

I'm not going to hurt you. (*To us.*) Spoons, mix, cake, oven – yes.

Mix, cake, spoons, oven – no.

Simple basic rules.

(*To a spoon.*) You do not ever get into the oven and shut the door.

JOHN: You're not interested in what we should want –

MUM: You're made of wood.

JOHN: You're telling us what we should want.

MUM: Which one of you's behind this?

JOHN: You're telling us happiness is eating cake.

MUM: Happiness is eating cake. Whose idea was it?

(*MUM looks up to see that TEA SPOON and TABLE SPOON have written 'JOHN' on the wall behind JOHN. JOHN stands in front of it, unaware of it, speaking to MUM. MUM is gob-smacked.*)

JOHN: You think happiness should be eating cake – and perhaps it should be – perhaps it is – but it's not making us happy. What does that mean? Does it mean that happiness is having cake in our lives, whether or not we want it? Are you putting us in a prison?

MUM: John.

JOHN: If you *tell* me I am happy in the prison, does that *make* me happy in the prison? Is happiness being happy in a prison rather than unhappy in a prison? Can happiness be a prison?

(*The UTENSILS are now getting back to their normal selves – some of them fill and cover the cake with chocolate buttercream.*)

MUM: John.

JOHN: Yes Mummy?

MUM: Did you shut the spoons in the oven?

JOHN: Yes I did. You see – and this is a fundamental point. None of the spoons or me actually like it when you make cake.

MUM: Why?

JOHN: Making cake doesn't make us happy.

MUM: Why did you put the spoons in the oven?

JOHN: I thought it would be fun to see them burn.

MUM: Fun?

JOHN: More fun than making cake.

MUM: I don't make cake for my own amusement.

JOHN: I think you'll find you do.

MUM: I'm doing this for you. We're making the cake together.

JOHN: We're not. You're making cake, I'm shutting the spoons in the oven and the spoons are getting hot.

MUM: The whole point of the cake is that it's for all of us.

JOHN: I think it's for your own personal satisfaction.

MUM: If I was going to do something for my own satisfaction, it would not be making cake.

JOHN: I don't think you should get angry.

MUM: Apologise to the spoons now.

JOHN: I won't.

MUM: Then get back in the cupboard.

JOHN: I just want to point out that you're putting a lot of effort into this cake for very little effect.

MUM: I'm going to say this once more.

JOHN: Very little effect.

MUM: Get in the cupboard, John.

JOHN: Is the cupboard the prison?

MUM: John.

JOHN: Or is the prison made of cake?

MUM: I'm going to count to three.

JOHN: No!

MUM: One, two –

JOHN: I don't like counting!

(*MUM grabs him and shuts him in the cupboard. She gets decorations out. The UTENSILS help her decorate the cake, and also decorate themselves with sugar eyes and hairstyles. Their movements are sometimes dance-like, sometimes they move like synchronized swimmers.*)

MUM: (*To us.*) You can really use your imagination when it comes to decorating your cake. As well as piping, you can add pieces of nut, silver balls, glace cherries, sugar flowers, sugar fruit, chocolate buttons, sweets,

crystallized flowers, grated chocolate –
(*We hear the cupboard door rattling.*)
A small bunch of redcurrants or some strawberries,
candied orange and lemon, sprinkles, vermicelli.
(*JOHN bangs on the cupboard door.*)
The trick with all of these decorations is to place them
on the cake when the frosting is thick enough to hold
them in place, but not quite firm. You don't want them
slipping about, or damaging your piping.
(*JOHN launches himself out of the cupboard and across the
room at MUM headfirst. MUM side-steps him and JOHN
ends up stuck in the flip-top bin which is sunk into the work
surface. MUM completely ignores him as he tries to get his
head out – struggling to release himself – lots of effort sounds.*)

JOHN: Why are we doing it?
(*As they continue, MUM finishes icing and decorating the
cake.*)

MUM: You can always use a blob of buttercream to hold
your decorations in place.

JOHN: If this cake is making none of us happy, why are we
here?
(*The UTENSILS come to have a look at JOHN.*)

MUM: (*To JOHN.*) It's not the cake itself – it's the cake
event.

JOHN: The event of making the cake, which we do not
participate in – I'm stuck in the bin, Mummy.
(*MUM goes over to JOHN. She very much wants to finish
the cake – and returns to it whenever she can.
They continue talking as MUM starts to haul him out – by
pulling on his body. The UTENSILS find this difficult
viewing, some turn away.*)
We can pretend to be happy – aah!

MUM: It's all right.

JOHN: But will we find happiness by pretending to be
happy?

MUM: All right – Mummy's here.

JOHN: If I pretend to be happy, will you be happy? If you
get what you want?

MUM: You're nearly out.

(*MUM is pulling very hard now.*)

JOHN: My head!

(*Pop: JOHN comes out of the bin – but his head has fallen into it. The UTENSILS are very shocked. MUM sits JOHN down, doesn't seem perturbed. JOHN doesn't notice he has no head. The spoons drift closer to JOHN.*)

Is there no more to happiness than getting what you want?

(*A spoon looks down JOHN's neck and he realises he has no head.*)

My head!

MUM: Okay –

JOHN: Where's my head?

MUM: I'll get your head.

JOHN: Where's my head?

MUM: Sit there a minute.

JOHN: My fucking bastard head!

MUM: John, don't say fucking bastard.

(*She grabs one of the petrified UTENSILS who have gathered round – the braver ones peering down into JOHN's neck, looking for his head. She uses the UTENSIL to lever the head out of the bin. MUM puts the UTENSIL and the head down on the worktop as she puts the final touches to the cake. As she continues, the UTENSIL gets up with JOHN's head on its head, running around. The other UTENSILS are fascinated but terrified.*)

Right.

JOHN: My head – that's my head – give it me – I want my head!

MUM: In a tin, this cake will keep up to a week, but there's nothing like the taste of a freshly baked cake, still moist with warmth.

(*The UTENSIL stops and looks at JOHN's body.*)

JOHN: Give me my head –

(*TEA SPOON comes over and takes JOHN's head from the other spoon. It goes over and starts to put it back on JOHN's body as MUM continues. Other UTENSILS help.*)

MUM: There are no rules about eating cake, aside from good common sense – not to eat a whole cake at one sitting. I like to swallow each mouthful before I've quite chewed it enough, but that's personal taste.

JOHN: (*To the UTENSILS.*) Thank you.

(*TEA SPOON moves JOHN's hair out of his eyes. They look at each other – a peace has been made. The cake is finished.*)

MUM: There. It's ready.

(*MUM places it in the centre of the worktop, with pride. She takes a deep breath and let it out again. Music starts.*)

Whether it's to be enjoyed with family or friends, for a special occasion or just for tea – a cake says something that savories, biscuits – even words can't.

Scene 5

As MUM continues, SPOONS gather. First the old favourites, then more and more. They all have cake-decoration faces, some have cake-ruff skirts and ribbons. All crowding round. All keen. Until there is a crowd.

MUM: You might not think you need a sharp knife to cut cake – but make the mistake of using a blunt one and your beautifully decorated topping will be dragged down through the sponge.

JOHN: What will we do after we've eaten the cake? Will we all live happily ever after?

MUM: (*To JOHN.*) I think we'll go to bed. (*To us.*) Your lovely light sponge will be compressed, pulling the two halves apart and making for a very unappealing slice.

JOHN: Because it seems to me that even if the cake does make us happy, that happiness may not last.

(*The crowds part to let a SHARP KNIFE through – like a bouncer at a gig. MUM picks it up and starts to slice the cake as spoons crowd round.*)

MUM: (*To the KNIFE.*) Hold tight.

JOHN: That want for the cake may be replaced by another want. By the want for another cake.

MUM: (*To the UTENSILS.*) No need to push. (*To JOHN.*) Here's your slice, John.

(*MUM gives JOHN his slice, then keeps cutting, UTENSILS*)

cluster round. MUM addresses us and the UTENSILS as JOHN tries to eat the cake.)
(*To the UTENSILS.*) Let me cut it up – hang on. (*To us.*) A round cake should be cut from the centre out –

JOHN: (*To us.*) It's not going in.

(As JOHN continues, a few UTENSILS register what's happening to him. This news is passed through the crowd – MUM doesn't realise.)

MUM: So your cuts are like spokes on a wheel.

JOHN: (*To us.*) I'm trying, but it's not going in.

MUM: And your slices wider at the edge than the centre.

JOHN: (*To us.*) If I've got a mouth and I can't eat cake, how can the spoons eat cake when they haven't got mouths?

MUM: Whereas a square cake is best cut across.

JOHN: (*To the UTENSILS and us.*) I can't eat it.

MUM: And then along.

(MUM finishes cutting and puts the KNIFE down.)
(*To the KNIFE.*) You stay still – I don't want anyone getting hurt.

JOHN: Mummy, the event of the cake is somewhat undermined by the fact that we cannot eat the cake. We can pretend to eat the cake, but we cannot eat the cake you have made.

MUM: I made the cake because I love you.

JOHN: Are there not other expressions of love? I love you mummy.

MUM: I love you.

(TEA SPOON brings her a mouthful of cake. She leans down and takes it with her mouth – chews and swallows, although it sticks in her throat.)

JOHN: I love you very much.

MUM: I would die for you, John.

JOHN: And I would eat cake for you, Mummy, if I could.

(A UTENSIL keels over with tiredness. As JOHN and MUM continue, more and more keel over – the crowd is disappearing.)
Is it very late, Mummy?

MUM: Yes, John, it's very late.

(MUM catches UTENSILS when they fall over with tiredness and puts them quickly into their drawer – sometimes kissing

*one as she does so, or holding one to her for a moment. JOHN
and MUM speak to us.)*

JOHN: What is cake, Mummy?

MUM: It's a foodstuff, John. It's lots of good things mixed together in such a way that bad things go away.

JOHN: Are you saying there's no bad in cake?

MUM: Apart from a bit of sugar. And a bit of sugar's not bad in the same way that betrayal or the wholesale slaughter of innocent people or abuse of power are bad.

JOHN: What's the wholesale slaughter of innocent people?

MUM: Well it's, well –

JOHN: Is it a foodstuff, Mummy?

(MUM is putting JOHN in a tea-towel bed.)

MUM: No it's not, John.

(She pulls back the covers.)

In you get.

JOHN: Do I have to, Mummy?

MUM: Yes you do.

(He gets into bed.)

JOHN: Only I'm not actually tired.

MUM: I think you are, John.

(He continues talking, propped on one arm.)

JOHN: Is making cake a good thing, Mummy?

MUM: I've always made cake.

JOHN: Is it the best thing?

MUM: The best foodstuff?

JOHN: The best thing, Mummy.

*(Lights are just on MUM, JOHN and the cake now. MUM
looks at the cake.)*

Do you feel despair, Mummy?

MUM: I don't know.

JOHN: Does it seem like there's no answer?

MUM: Night night, John.

JOHN: Night night.

*(JOHN stirs as he gets comfortable in his sleep. She loves
them all so much. Light remains on the cake for a moment.
Then goes.)*

www.ingramcontent.com/pod-product-compliance
Ingram Content Group UK Ltd.
Pitfield, Milton Keynes, MK11 3LW, UK
UKHW020723280225
455688UK00012B/481